YACHTMASTER EXERCISES
FOR SAIL & POWER

5th edition

YACHTMASTER EXERCISES
FOR SAIL & POWER

Questions and answers for the RYA Yachtmaster® Certificates of Competence

ALISON NOICE AND ROGER SEYMOUR

LONDON • OXFORD • NEW YORK • NEW DELHI • SYDNEY

ADLARD COLES
Bloomsbury Publishing Plc
50 Bedford Square, London, WC1B 3DP, UK
29 Earlsfort Terrace, Dublin 2, Ireland

BLOOMSBURY, ADLARD COLES and the Adlard Coles logo are trademarks of
Bloomsbury Publishing Plc

First published in Great Britain 2005
Second edition 2010
Third edition 2012
Fourth edition 2018
This edition published 2024

Copyright © Alison Noice, 2010, 2012, 2018
Copyright © Roger Seymour, 2024

Alison Noice and Roger Seymour have asserted their rights under the Copyright,
Designs and Patents Act, 1988, to be identified as Authors of this work

For legal purposes the Acknowledgements on p. vi
constitute an extension of this copyright page

All rights reserved. No part of this publication may be reproduced or transmitted in any form or by any means,
electronic or mechanical, including photocopying, recording, or any information storage or retrieval system,
without prior permission in writing from the publishers

Bloomsbury Publishing Plc does not have any control over, or responsibility for,
any third-party websites referred to or in this book. All internet addresses given in this
book were correct at the time of going to press. The author and publisher regret any
inconvenience caused if addresses have changed or sites have ceased to exist,
but can accept no responsibility for any such changes

A catalogue record for this book is available from the British Library

Library of Congress Cataloguing-in-Publication data has been applied for

ISBN: PB: 978-1-3994-0992-6

2 4 6 8 10 9 7 5 3 1

Typeset in Myriad Pro by Rod Teasdale
Printed and bound in India by Replika Press Pvt. Ltd.

To find out more about our authors and books visit www.bloomsbury.com and sign up for our newsletters

Note: While all reasonable care has been taken in the publication of this book, the publisher takes no
responsibility for the use of the methods or products described in the book. Extracts from navigational sources
are included for practice only, are not to be considered up to date and must not be used for navigation.

Yachtmaster is a trademark of the Royal Yachting Association registered in the United Kingdom and
selected marketing territories

CONTENTS

Acknowledgements vi
Introduction vii

EXERCISES — 1

1. Charts 1
2. Compass 2
3. Position Fixing 4
4. Buoys, Lights and Lighthouses 6
5. Tidal Heights 8
6. Tidal Streams 11
7. Course to Steer 13
8. Dead Reckoning and Estimated Position 15
9. Electronic navigation and instruments 17
10. Pilotage 19
11. Collision Regulations 22
12. Meteorology 25
13. Safety and Communications 28
14. Planning and Making Passages 31

CHARTWORK TEST PAPERS — 35

15. Test Paper 1 35
16. Test Paper 2 36

ANSWERS (SECTIONS 1 TO 14 AND TEST PAPERS 1 AND 2) — 37–88

EXTRACTS — 89

1. Tides: Dover, May to August 89
2. Tides: Dover, September to December 90
3. Tidal Streams, based on HW Dover 91
4. Tidal Streams, based on HW Dover 92
5. Tides: St Helier 93
6. Port Information: St Helier 94
7. Tidal Curves: St Helier 95
8. Tidal Curves: Cherbourg 96
9. Tides: Cherbourg 97
10. Tides: St Malo 98
11. Tidal Curves: St Malo 99
12. Port Information: St Malo 100
13. Port Information: St Peter Port 101
14. Port Information: Granville and Îles Chausey 102
15. Port Information: Diélette 103
16. Deviation Curve 104
17. Tidal Differences for Cherbourg–Barfleur 104

ACKNOWLEDGEMENTS

My grateful thanks go to the following people who have helped with this book, and the companies who willingly gave permission for use of their material:

Adlard Coles

International Maritime Organisation

Longbow Sail Training

Maritime & Coastguard Agency

McMurdo

Pains Wessex

Raymarine

Reeds Nautical Almanac

Roger Seymour

Royal Yachting Association

Simrad

Stanford Maritime

UK Hydrographic Office

Special thanks to Peter Noice, who took many photographs and constantly nursed my computer with never-ending patience.

INTRODUCTION

This book of exercises has been written to give student navigators the chance to perfect chartwork and seamanship skills learned from books such as *Yachtmaster for Sail and Power* or from RYA navigation courses. The saying 'practice makes perfect' may sound trite, but it is infinitely preferable to get to grips with a subject in a warm, secure classroom than when the wind and sea are making life uncomfortable!

The subjects covered in the exercises are those in the RYA Coastal and Yachtmaster syllabus, and each exercise is graded with the more complex questions at the end. A Stanfords Channel Island chart has been included for the chartwork and passage-planning exercises; this has proved ideal for the job as it gives a variety of places to visit, and rocky channels for pilotage problems.

The comprehensive step-by-step answer section explains how a solution has been achieved and should help establish an order of work when solving problems involving tidal height and course to steer. Emphasis has been placed on the use of modern electronic equipment without neglecting the vital traditional skills that need to be used in conjunction with them.

Finally, remember that all this theoretical knowledge needs to be put to good use where it matters most – out on the water. A few days spent navigating a boat on a coastal cruise is of more value than weeks spent in the classroom. There is nothing that surpasses the joyous feeling of entering a peaceful harbour after a tricky but safe passage with good friends as crew. After all, isn't that why you bought this book in the first place?

Alison Noice

This book was originally written by my dear friend and colleague Allison to enhance, complement and encourage all to practice their skills gained from *Yachtmaster for Sail and Power*.

I have endeavoured to retain her unique style and humour whilst updating electronics, safety, communications to those used today in navigation.

The basic chartwork skills remain the same whether you draw lines on a paper or electronic chart. Remember practice makes perfect.

Roger Seymour

EXERCISES • CHARTS

1 CHARTS

You will require the chart to answer some of these questions.

1.1
In which Admiralty publication will you find all the symbols used on paper and electronic charts?

1.2
Looking at the Channel Islands chart would you expect the charted depth in the darker blue area to be more or less than 10 metres?

1.3
Explain what feature is in position:

a) 49°42'.8N 002°08'.5W

b) 49°44'.6N 001°44'.0W

c) 48°58'.2N 002°19'.3W

d) 49°30'.1N 002°30'.0W

1.4
You will find Grand Léjon light in position 48°45'.0N 002°39'.8W.

Explain the full meaning of the associated caption.

1.5
a) Which datum is used for the positions on the Channel Islands chart?

b) Which datum is used for most electronic charts?

1.6
Is a straight line drawn on a Mercator chart:

a) a great circle?   OR   b) a rhumb line?

1.7
What are the precise meanings of the following chart symbols?

     e) f)   j)

1.8
Do most marine chartplotters use vector or raster charts?

1.9
What is the difference between a raster scan chart and a vector chart?

2 COMPASS

2.1
The notation on the compass rose of a chart states:

Variation 3°20′W (2019) decreasing 8′ annually

What will the variation be in 2024?

2.2
A compass can suffer from deviation. Explain the meaning of this statement. What are some of the possible causes of deviation?

2.3
Your autopilot is fitted with an electronic compass. Is this device subject to deviation?

2.4
You are at a boat jumble looking for a new steering compass for your fast sports boat. The vendor tells you that the one he is offering has been taken off a small yacht.

Will it be suitable for your boat? Give reasons.

2.5
You are south-east of Grand Léjon (south-western corner of the practice chart) and wish to fix your position using a hand-bearing compass.

Would you expect to get an accurate fix? Give reasons.

2.6
What is the MAGNETIC bearing for each of the following?

a) 065°T variation 5°W
b) 005°T variation 8°E
c) 247°T variation 15°E
d) 357°T variation 4°W

2.7
What is the TRUE bearing for each of the following?

a) 135°M variation 12°W
b) 315°M variation 10°E
c) 002°M variation 3°W
d) 180°M variation 6°E

EXERCISES • COMPASS

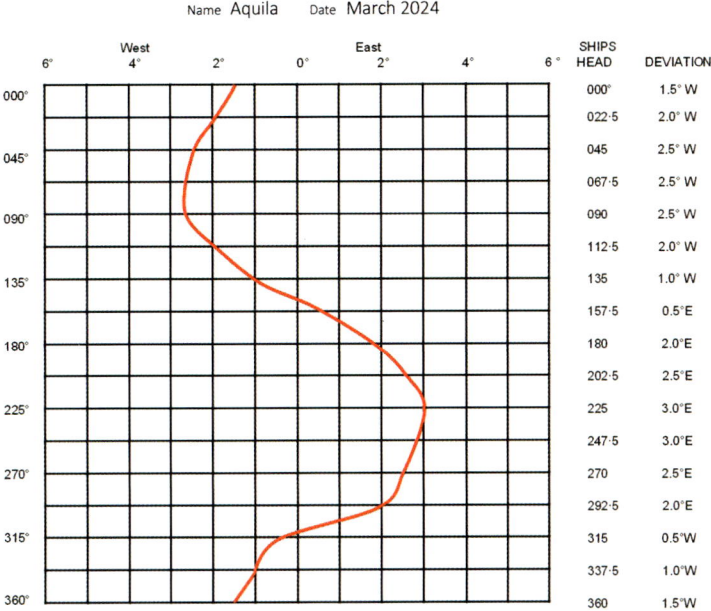

Fig 2.1 Deviation card.

2.8

The variation is 3°W. Calculate the TRUE course using the deviation card in Fig 2.1 for each of the following:

a) 180°C

b) 146°C

c) 225°C

d) 338°C

2.9

A helmsman is approaching St Helier, Jersey, from the south keeping the Oc R and the Oc G leading lights in transit. The tidal stream is slack and the magnetic variation is 3°W.

What is the deviation if the compass is reading 023°C?

2.10

A helmsman is approaching Guernsey from the south-east, keeping the Lower Heads South Cardinal Buoy in transit with the Al WR (alternating white and red) light on St Peter Port's breakwater. The stream is slack and the magnetic variation is 3°W.

What is the deviation if the compass reading is 309°C? (Use the inset chart on the left-hand side of the practice chart.)

2.11

When an electronic compass is installed in a boat why does it require calibration?

3 POSITION FIXING

Plot the fixes on the practice chart using 3°W variation.

3.1

At 1000, the following bearings were taken to the west of Jersey.

Corbière Lighthouse	133°M
Lookout Tower	035°M
White building	081°M

Plot the fix and give the latitude and longitude.

3.2

At 1630 the navigator of a small vessel on passage around the north-west corner of Jersey notices that the visibility is deteriorating rapidly but manages to take the following bearings before the fog closes in.

Lookout Tower south of Grosnez Point 064°M.
Tower about 0.7M south of Lookout 092°M.
Depth reduced to datum 3.1m. Cliffs look over a mile away.

Plot the fix and give the geographical position. Comment on the accuracy of this fix.

3.3

In moderate visibility a navigator has used Corbière Lighthouse as a GPS waypoint to make the plotting of GPS positions simple.

At 1500 Corbière Lighthouse bears 337°T 3.5M.

Plot the fix and give the answer as a bearing and distance from Noirmont Point light.

3.4

At 1800, the following fixes were taken to the south of Jersey.

Noirmont Point light in transit with Chimney to the east of St Helier 086°M.
Corbière Light 051°M.

Plot the fix and give the latitude and longitude.

3.5

On a glorious sunny day on passage near the southeast corner of the Îles Chausey, the crew advises the navigator that Le Pignon East Cardinal Mark is coming into transit with Le Haute Fouraine East Cardinal Mark, so she takes a quick bearing of Les Huguenans isolated danger mark as they come into line. The bearing is 278°M at 1430.

Plot the fix. How could the position be confirmed?

EXERCISES • POSITION FIXING

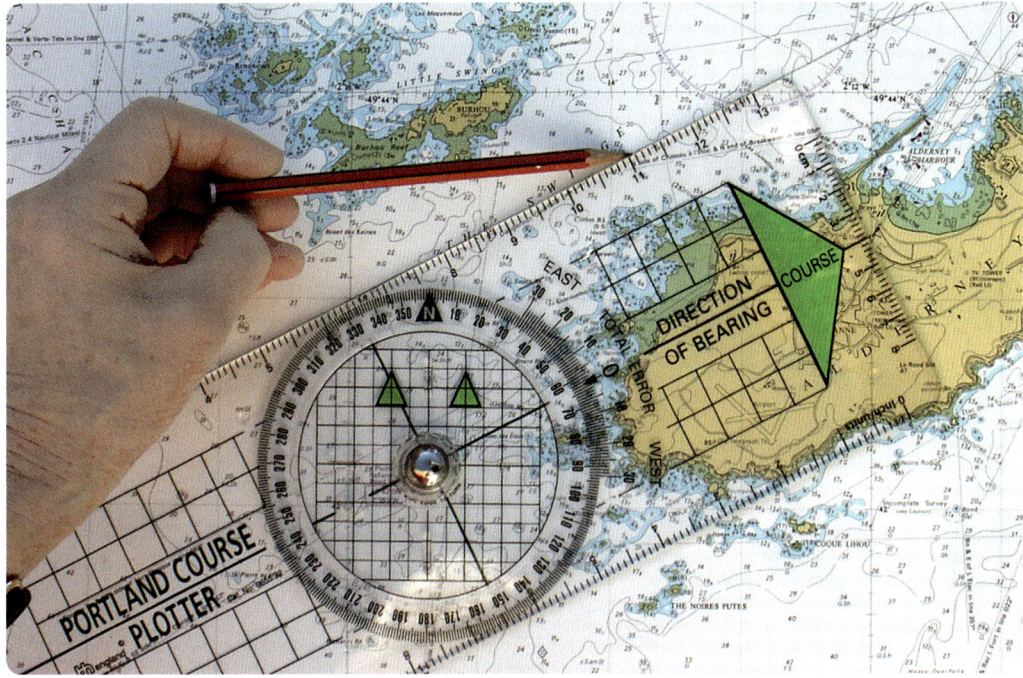

Marking a position line to plot a fix.

3.6

A boat with no GPS is on passage between St Malo and Granville on a night when the forecast is for fog. About halfway through the passage, the boat enters a fog bank but the skipper decides to continue towards Granville while keeping an accurate plot.

Later, at 0215, the fog clears in the local area and the depth sounder reads 14m (reduced to CD). At the same time, the following lights can be seen:

a) *To port*   An occulting white light with a 4-second sequence.

b) *Ahead*   A white light, very weak and difficult to see above the waves. One crew member thinks that it has nine flashes. It is difficult to take an accurate bearing of the buoy but it is thought to be within 5 degrees of 075°M.

Plot the boat's approximate position and draw the area of uncertainty.

Would it be safe to approach Granville if the fog comes down again?

4. BUOYS, LIGHTS AND LIGHTHOUSES

4.1
There are two international buoyage systems – IALA A and IALA B.

a) Which system is used in Europe and much of the world?

b) What is the main difference between the two systems?

4.2
Using the Channel Islands chart, identify the type of buoy or beacon:

a) in position 49°41'.3N 001°44'.4W.

b) in position 48°53'.6N 002°55'.2W.

4.3
What is the significance of the three buoys in the illustration below?

What is the colour and sequence of the light on each?

 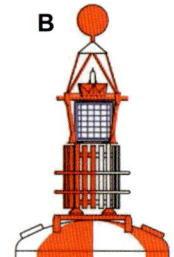 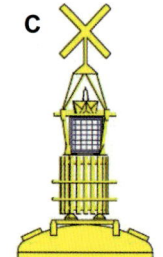

Fig 4.1 Buoys.

4.4
Explain the difference between a *flashing*, an *occulting* and an *isophase* light.

4.5
a) Which of the two posts in Fig 4.2 should be inserted at the division of the two channels if the one to the right were the preferred channel?

b) What colour light would this post have?

c) What would be the sequence of the light?

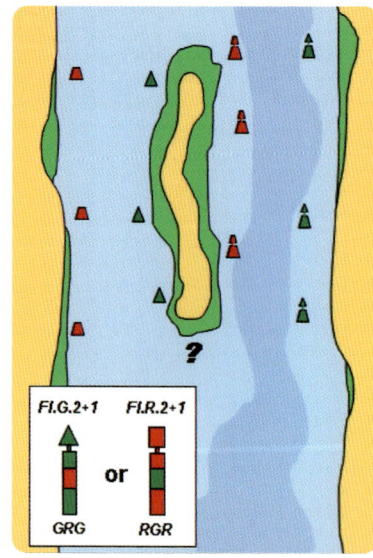

Fig 4.2 Channel buoyage.

4.6

The leading lights into St Malo are described as FG.

a) What is the meaning of this abbreviation?

b) Would you expect to be able to see these lights from Le Vieux Banc if the visibility was good?

4.7

From a position 48°40'.6N 002°37'.4W (in the Baie de Saint-Brieuc) what colour light would be seen from:

a) the Grand Léjon light?

b) the Rohein light?

c) the Erquy leading light?

4.8

Point Corbière Lighthouse on the south-west corner of Jersey is shown as having the following characteristics:

Iso WR 10s 36m 18/16M Horn Mo (C) 60s

Describe *in full* what this means.

4.9

What are the advantages and or disadvantages of AIS navigation marks?

Fig 4.3 Point Corbière Light, Jersey.

5 TIDAL HEIGHTS

5.1

Which of the letters in the illustration (Fig 5.1) refer to the following?

i) Chart datum
ii) MHWS
iii) Clearance height
iv) Depth of water
v) MLWN
vi) Charted depth
vii) Height of tide
viii) MLWS
ix) HAT
x) Charted height
xi) MHWN
xii) Drying height

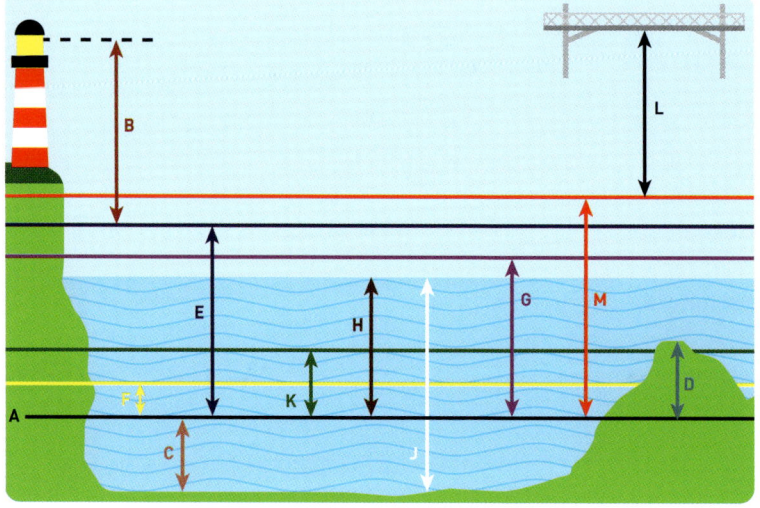

Fig 5.1 Tide levels.

5.2

The height of tide at St Malo is calculated at 6.8m.

a) Using the large-scale chart of St Malo at the bottom of the chart, what is the depth of water just south of the marina at Dinard?

b) What is the depth of water in position 48°40′.5N 002°01′.6W?

5.3

Use the tidal information given for St Malo in Fig 5.2, the chart and the port information for St Malo in the extracts section to answer the following:

a) What will be the height of Les Bas-Sablons light above the water at MLWN?

b) What will be the depth of water close to the ferry terminal in St Malo at MLWS?

c) A skipper of a yacht with an air draught of 17.0m wishes to pass under a bridge in the River Rance at St Malo. This bridge is charted as having a clearance height of 20m. What clearance will there be above the mast at MHWS?

d) A boat drawing 2.2m anchors close to St Malo at MHWN. What will be the clearance under the keel at MLWN if the depth of water when he anchored was 8.0m?

EXERCISES • TIDAL HEIGHTS

Standard Port ST MALO

Height (metres)

HAT	MHWS	MHWN	MLWN	MLWS
13.6	12.2	9.3	4.2	1.5

Fig 5.2 St Malo tidal information

5.4

In what way could a high barometric pressure affect the heights of tide?

5.5

What will be the height of tide at 1357 on Saturday 4 September at St Helier?

5.6

Use the information given in Extract 13 to answer this question.

The skipper of a boat that draws 1.8m wishes to enter the marina in St Peter Port. HW 1544 7.4m. What is the earliest time he can enter the marina with a 0.3m clearance under the keel?

5.7

It is 0930 on Saturday 5 June when a boat with a draught of 1.5m develops engine trouble off St Malo. The skipper manages to anchor very close to the 1.1m drying height just outside Les Bas-Sablons Marina. The tide is falling so the skipper decides to calculate the latest time by which he must complete the repairs in order to avoid a grounding.

What is the latest time he must leave with a minimum of 1.5m under the keel?

5.8

What are the times and heights of high and low water at Saint-Vaast-la-Hougue during the afternoon and evening on Sunday 12 September?

Hint: Note that a time difference of +0115 means 1 hour and 15 minutes.

Standard Port CHERBOURG

Times				Height (metres)			
High Water		Low Water		MHWS	MHWN	MLWN	MLWS
0300	1000	0400	1000	6.4	5.1	2.6	1.1
1500	2200	1600	2200				
Differences ST VAAST-LA-HOUGUE							
+0115	+0045	+0120	+0110	+0.3	+0.3	-0.2	-0.1

5.9

What are the times and heights of high and low water at Braye (Alderney) during the middle of the day on Thursday 9 December?

5.10

At 1545 on Thursday 22 July a yacht grounds just outside Diélette on the western side of the Cherbourg peninsula.

a) What are the times and heights of HW and the height of LW at Diélette in the middle of the day on 22 July? Give the answer in local time.

b) What is the height of tide when she grounds?

c) At what time will she float again later in the evening?

5.11

The skipper of a bilge-keel yacht drawing 1.5m wishes to dry out at Îles Chausey to repair the rudder. He anchors in a depth of 2.5m at 1000 on Tuesday 15 June.

a) What is the height of tide at 1000?

b) At what time will the boat ground?

c) When will it dry out completely so that work can begin?

d) At what time will the water reach the keel again in the afternoon?

Waiting for the tide at Emsworth.

6 TIDAL STREAMS

Use the tidal diamond information given on the practice chart and the tidal stream charts at the back of the book. Times vary from question to question.

6.1

Use the course plotter and the tidal stream chartlets in the extracts section to find the direction and rate of the tidal stream:

a) Off Portrieux, 2 hours before HW Dover at neaps.

b) Along the north-east corner of Jersey, 4 hours after HW Dover at springs.

c) North of Cherbourg, 4 hours before HW Dover, midway between neaps and springs.

6.2

Use a course plotter and the tidal stream chartlets at the back of this book to find the direction and rate of the tidal stream:

a) Just north of St Malo between 0252 and 0352 BST on Tuesday 7 September.

b) Close to the east of Guernsey between 0730 and 0830 BST on Saturday 16 October.

c) On the north-east corner of Jersey between 1744 and 1844 UTC on Monday 1 November.

For information: Dover ranges – springs 6.0m, neaps 3.2m.

6.3

Use the data for diamond ◇L◇ from the tidal stream panel at the bottom of the chart to determine the direction and rate of the tidal stream:

a) HW St Helier +5hrs at springs.

b) HW St Helier –2hrs at neaps.

c) HW St Helier –6hrs midway between neaps and springs.

6.4

Use tidal diamond ◇E◇ to find the direction and rate of the tidal stream to the west of Guernsey:

a) Between 0958 and 1058 local time on Thursday 16 September.

b) Between 0728 and 0828 local time on Monday 8 November.

c) Between 1823 and 1923 local time on Tuesday 19 October.

6.5

Using the tidal stream atlas, at what time (BST) during the afternoon of Saturday 25 September is the tide slack to the east of Portrieux?

6.6

On Friday 1 October it is intended to make passage between Cherbourg and Guernsey in a light-displacement motor cruiser that is capable of 30kn. The weather forecast is for SW Force 3/4 winds.

Between what times (BST) will the sea be most calm during the morning?

6.7

When planning a passage, what is meant by the phrase 'tidal gate'?

6.8

Are the following phrases TRUE or FALSE?

a) The stream is weakest in shallow water.

b) The range of the tide is never more than the mean range given in the almanac.

c) The tidal stream can change direction at any time relative to local HW and LW.

d) The sea is roughest in a wind-against-tide situation.

e) The tidal stream runs strongly at neaps and is weaker at springs.

f) The stream around a prominent headland is usually stronger than along straight coastlines.

Evening calm in Kalkan, Turkey.

7 COURSE TO STEER

Use the practice chart and extracts at the back of the book. Use 3°W variation. Time zones vary from question to question.

7.1

At 1600, a boat is in position 49°06′.8N 02°09′.4W. The skipper intends to enter St Helier harbour (Jersey) and wishes to approach using the leading line. The boat speed is 5kn.

What is the magnetic course to steer to remain on the line while counteracting a tidal stream of 315°T 1.5kn?

7.2

At 1800 a fishing boat weighs anchor from a position 48°50′.4N 002°05′.5W. The skipper intends to enter St Malo using the Chenal de la Petite Porte. The boat speed is 17kn and the tidal stream 108°T 1.5kn.

a) What is the magnetic course to steer to the safe water mark to the north-west of the port?

b) What will be the time when he gets to this position?

7.3

At 1300 a racing yacht is in position 48°49′.4N, 002°15′.8W sailing on a broad reach at 10 knots.

The tidal stream: 1230–1330 097°T 1.8kn
1330–1430 084°T 1.6kn

a) What is the course to steer to a position 0.3M west of Banchenou starboard-hand mark at the entrance to the Chenal de la Grande Porte?

b) If the position of the destination was entered as a waypoint in the GPS, how would it be possible to see if the boat were on the intended ground track?

7.4

At 1340 BST on Sunday 17 October, a boat is in a position 1M due south of L'Etac rock on Sark, making for Désormes West Cardinal Mark, north of Jersey.

a) What is the time of HW St Helier? What is the range? Is it neaps or springs?

b) Using diamond ◇J◇, what will be the tidal stream between 1340 and 1440?

c) What is the magnetic course to steer to the buoy if the boat speed is 8kn?

d) At what time will the boat reach the buoy?

7.5

At 1405 BST on Thursday 28 October a cruiser is in position 49°20'.6N 002°25'.6W bound for St Peter Port. She is logging 15kn.

a) What is the time of HW St Helier? Is it neaps or springs?

b) Using tidal diamond ⟨J⟩ what will be the tidal stream during the passage?

c) What will be the magnetic course to steer to a position 0.2M west of the SCM south of Herm Island?

d) Approximately how long will it take to reach the buoy?

7.6

On Sunday 5 September, a yacht is sailing at 5kn well heeled on starboard tack (wind blowing from the starboard side). At 1628, she is between Sark and Jersey in position 49°18'.6N 002°20'.0W.

a) Use the tidal stream charts to calculate the magnetic course to steer for a point 239°T from Grosnez Point lighthouse 2.8M.

b) If the yacht were making 10° leeway, what would be the magnetic course to steer?

7.7

A boat has NE Minquiers East Cardinal Mark entered into the GPS as a waypoint for plotting positions, and the position given on the display at 1130 BST on Friday 17 September is 139°M 2.0M to the buoy.

a) Using tidal diamond ⟨N⟩ and the deviation curve in the extracts section, calculate the compass course to steer for the Mo (D) WR light outside St Helier if the boat speed is 7kn.

b) What will be the course over ground (COG) and the speed over ground (SOG)?

c) What will be the ETA at the light?

8 DEAD RECKONING AND ESTIMATED POSITION

Use the extracts section for tidetables, tidal stream charts, deviation card and harbour information. Use variation 3°W. Time zones vary from question to question.

8.1

Use the following information to plot the dead reckoning (DR) position at 1500.

1400	Close to Oc(3)12s light near Binic.
	Log reads 0.0M. Steering 074°M.
1430	Log reads 4.1M. Alter course to 061°M.
1500	Log reads 8.1M. Anchored for diving.

Plot the position at 1500. What is the feature at the DR position?

8.2

At 1800 a small fishing boat weighs anchor in position 48°41′.85N 002°36′.5W and sets a course of 125°M at 5kn.

The tidal stream for the next hour is 263°T 1.4kn.

a) Plot the estimated position (EP) at 1900 and give the latitude and longitude.

b) What is the true course over ground (COG)?

c) What is the speed over ground (SOG)?

8.3

Fig 8.1 is an extract from the logbook of a motor cruiser on passage. Plot the EP at 1430 and express the position as a true bearing and distance to a waypoint at Men-Marc'h East Cardinal Beacon.

Time	Course	Log	Wind	L/Way	Baro	Depth	Notes
1400	000°M	1.9	S2	nil	1032	11.0m	0.4M west of Madeux Bn.
1430	000°M	14.0	S2	nil	1032	26.0m	Choppy water. EP plotted using tidal stream 160°T 2.4kn.

Fig 8.1 Logbook extract.

8.4

At 1037 BST on Thursday 30 September, a yacht is in position 48°41′.4N 02°47′.8W, steering a course of 035°M. The distance log reads 3.2M at 1037.

a) What is the time of HW Dover? Is it springs or neaps?
b) Using the tidal stream charts, what is the direction and rate of the stream between 1037 and 1137?
c) Plot the EP at 1137 BST when the log reads 9.0M.
d) What is the COG and SOG?

8.5

At 0700, a yacht is in position 49°09′.8N 02°45′.8W, sailing close-hauled on a heading of 245°M, and the skipper is aiming to sail to the west of Plateau des Roches-Douvres. Unfortunately, the neap stream is east-going so he decides to plot a projected EP to determine whether he will be clear of the danger area. He has calculated the tidal stream as 110°T 1.6kn and his average boat speed is 5½kn.

a) Plot the projected EP for 0800 and give the latitude and longitude.
b) Will the yacht be clear of the danger area?

8.6

Fig 8.2 is an extract from the logbook of a boat on passage from Saint-Quay-Portrieux to St Malo on Tuesday 23 November. Plot the EP at 1538 UTC.

Tuesday 23 November. Time Zone UTC.							
Time	Course	Log	Wind	L/Way	Baro	Depth	Notes
1338	060°M	6.7	W3	nil	1005	17.0m	Position: 48°40′.0N 02°37′.6W
1425	060°M	11.0	W4	nil	1006	17.0m	A/C 095°M near Les Landas NCM
1538	095°M	18.6	W4	nil	1006	18.0m	EP plotted using ®

Fig 8.2 Logbook extract.

8.7

A yacht is on passage from Jersey to Saint-Quay-Portrieux and is approaching the Baie de St Brieuc. At 0953 BST on Thursday 14 October the position is fixed by GPS with reference to a waypoint centred on Grand Léjon lighthouse.

a) If the position given at 0953 (log reading 31.3) is 245°T 3.9M, is the yacht to the east or to the west of Grand Léjon lighthouse?
b) The yacht is logging 5kn on a heading of 185°C, making 5° leeway in a SE wind. What will be the direction of the line to be drawn on the chart?
c) Using tidal diamond ◇, what will be the direction and rate of the tidal stream between 0953 and 1053?
d) Will Petit Léjon beacon be to port or starboard as it is passed? How close will it be?
e) If the boat speed and the tidal stream were to remain the same for the foreseeable future, would the yacht pass to the east of Caffa East Cardinal Beacon?

9 ELECTRONIC NAVIGATION AND INSTRUMENTS

9.1

The paddle wheel log is the type fitted to most small boats as standard. The majority are now fitted with a chart plotter, and this is the primary source of navigation even though the crew will have nautical charts on their phones.

a) When out of sight of land why might it be prudent for you to take hourly log readings?

b) Give two possible reasons why the log might give an inaccurate reading.

c) Which would give you most cause for concern – a log that is under-reading or one that is over-reading?

9.2

Why might your depth sounder give unreliable readings when:

a) in shallow water when the seabed is soft mud?

b) passing through the wake of a big ship?

9.3

You have bought a new VHF DSC radio which includes a GPS and an AIS receiver.

a) What is the meaning of the abbreviation AIS?

b) Will other craft be able to see your position overlaid on their chartplotter?

c) What information should you receive about another vessel?

d) Why is it prudent for leisure craft to turn an AIS transponder off when in harbour?

Longbow II enjoying the strong wind.

9.4

Is it best to have your GPS antenna mounted as high as possible on the mast or much lower down? Give reasons.

9.5

a) You are talking to a friend about his radar set, which he describes as being 'stabilised'. Does this mean that:
   i) the set is screwed firmly to the bulkhead?
   ii) when the boat yaws the picture will remain stable and not swing from side to side?
   iii) the antenna does not tip to compensate for the motion of the boat?

b) Which of the following will be the better reflector of radar beams?
   i) a large motor cruiser with a GRP hull?
   ii) a smaller motor cruiser with an aluminium hull?

c) Your radar has an 18in radar scanner in a radome and your friend has a motor cruiser with a 48in open array. Are you or your friend likely to have most difficulty identifying a narrow harbour entrance from a distance? Give reasons.

d) What is the theoretical radar horizon for an antenna mounted 9 metres high?

e) What is meant by the phrase 'north up' when referring to a radar display?

f) When fine tuning your radar on passage, which control to remove irritating seaway echoes would you use? Why should it be used with extreme caution?

9.6

With reference to radar, what is the meaning of the following abbreviations?

a) MARPA

b) CPA

c) TCPA

9.7

You are about to fit a radar to your boat. Do you have to inform any authority that you have installed the set?

9.8

How could you update the charts in a chartplotter?

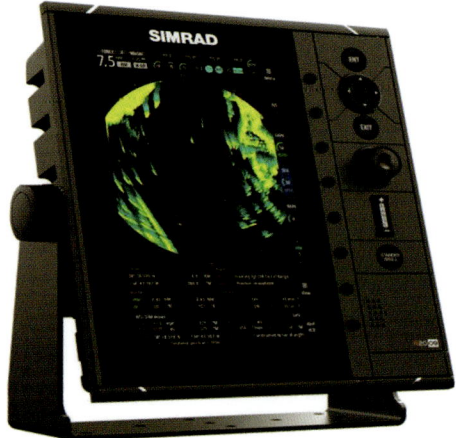

Fig 9.1 Simrad radar.

10 PILOTAGE

Use the extracts at the back of the book and inset charts on the practice chart where necessary. Use variation 3°W.

10.1

A boat is approaching Alderney from the south-west using the Swinge channel. The navigator is worried about hitting Corbet Rock and the off-lying rocks to the south-west of it.

a) Use the chart of Alderney in Figure 10.1 to suggest how major landmarks could be used to avoid the danger.

b) How can the pilot check when it is safe to turn and head straight for the end of the breakwater?

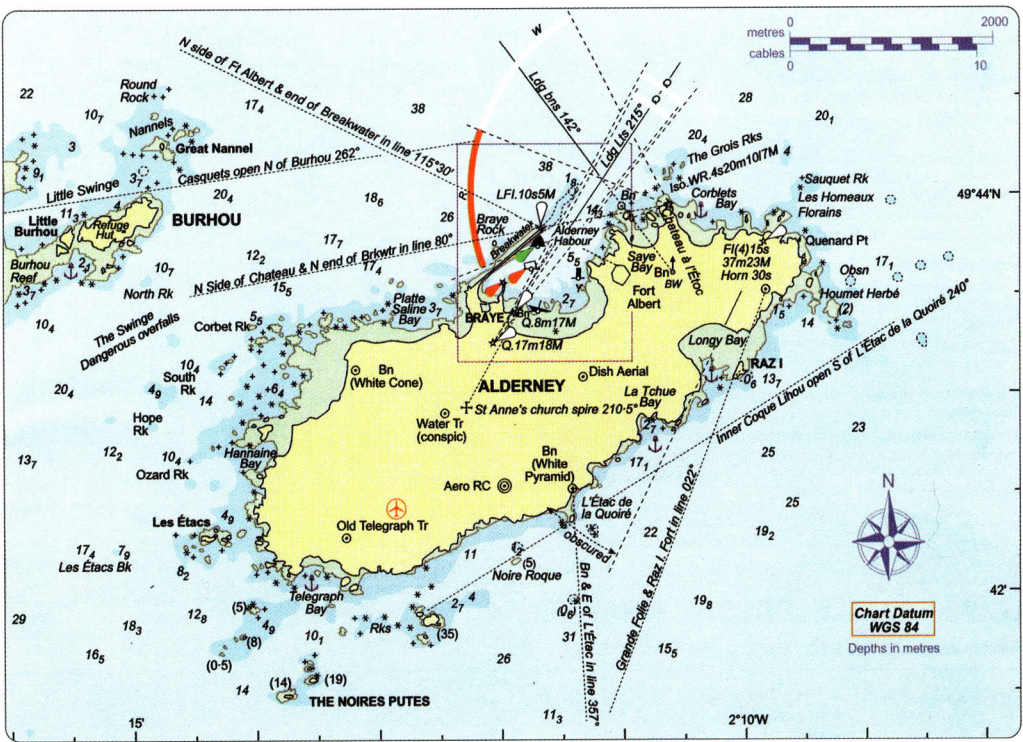

Fig 10.1 An extract from Stanfords Channel Island chart.

10.2

The skipper of a fast diving boat intends to return to Guernsey from Bouley Bay (north Jersey) after dark. The plan is to pass to the south of the Paternoster Rocks, and a waypoint at 49°16ʹ.7N 02°14ʹ.4W is entered into the portable GPS as part of the pilotage plan.

The boat gets underway and, once clear of the bay, the throttles are opened for a quick trip home. About 1½M short of the waypoint, one of the crew yells that he can see water breaking over a rock close to starboard.

a) What is the likely position?

b) What can have gone wrong with the plan?

c) How could the skipper have avoided this mistake?

10.3

A boat is leaving St Malo at night using the leading lights viewed from astern to navigate safely in the channel (see inset on lower edge of chart). As Le Grand Jardin lighthouse is approached, the helmsman announces that he will have to alter course to port to avoid hitting the lighthouse!

Will the configuration of the lights look like illustration a) or b) in Fig 10.2 when the boat is alongside the lighthouse?

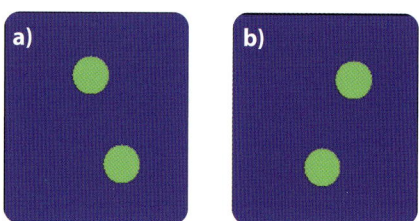

Fig 10.2 Which light configuration?

10.4

It is a perfect summer day in July with blue skies and a light breeze and ideal for a visit to Îles Chausey in a boat drawing 1.3m.

a) A crew member suggests visiting the bird sanctuary – is this allowed?

b) A boat arrives in Jersey from the UK then moves on to Îles Chausey. Is the skipper doing anything wrong?

c) Which VHF channel does the harbourmaster use?

d) Can you get a drink ashore on Chausey?

e) What minimum height of tide would be required for an exit via the north-western route if a 1.5m clearance under the keel is required?

10.5

A motor cruiser is preparing to enter the Bassin Vauban in St Malo. As the lock is approached, the skipper sees some lights on display (Fig 10.3).

What is the meaning of this signal? (See extracts section at the back of the book.)

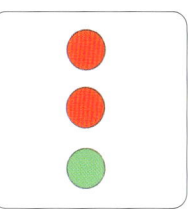

Fig 10.3 Lock lights.

10.6

A skipper planning to sail from Granville to St Malo on Sunday 20 June is preparing a pilotage plan and requires answers to the following questions:

a) Between which times during the morning (FSumT) is exit from the marina at Granville possible?

b) Why is care needed when leaving the marina?

c) Is it permitted to leave the marina under sail?

d) Where is the depth of water over the sill displayed?

e) The skipper decides to leave the marina as soon as the sill drops. What will the depth of water in the shallowest part of the entrance channel be at this time?

f) The yacht has a stiff sail to St Malo and arrives off Île Harbour at 1330. Is it possible for the yacht to pass over the sill into Les Bas-Sablons Marina at 1400 with a clearance of 1.0m or more under the keel?

g) On which VHF channel does the marina listen?

h) If the yacht got held up and missed the sill, is it possible to find anywhere to stop while waiting for the tide to rise again?

11 COLLISION REGULATIONS

11.1
To whom do the International Regulations for Preventing Collisions at Sea apply?

11.2
Do the collision regulations give one vessel the 'right of way' over another?

Explain your answer.

11.3
The illustrations in Fig 11.1 show situations where a risk of collision exists.

Which is the 'give way' vessel and what action should the skipper take?

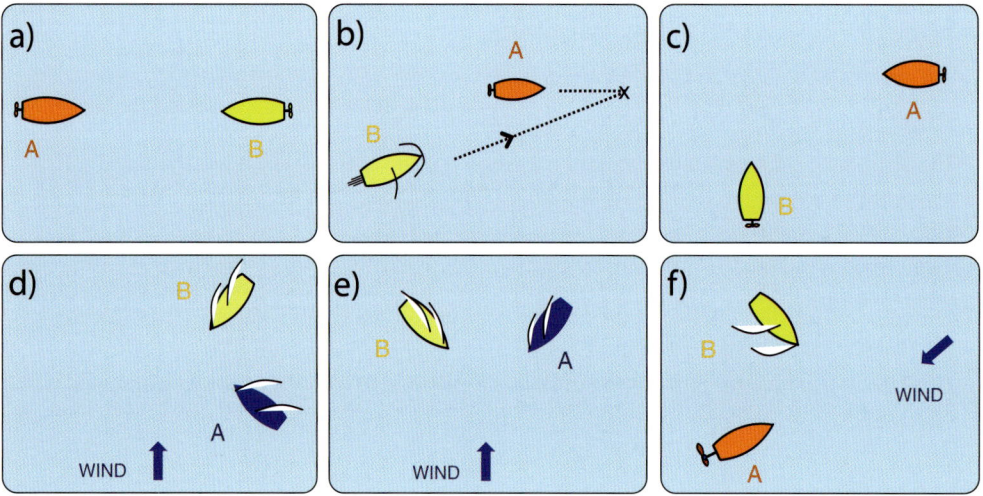

Fig 11.1 Collision risks.

11.4
According to the rules, what things should a skipper take into consideration when determining a safe speed? Mention four or more.

11.5
Which two types of craft are specifically forbidden to impede other larger craft when in a narrow channel?

11.6

You see the signal (shown in Fig 11.2) displayed on a vessel that is stopped.

What is the signal telling you?

Fig 11.2 Signal flag.

11.7

When crossing a Traffic Separation Scheme, should the ground track of the heading be at right angles to the separation lanes?

11.8

What is the meaning of the day shapes in Fig 11.3?

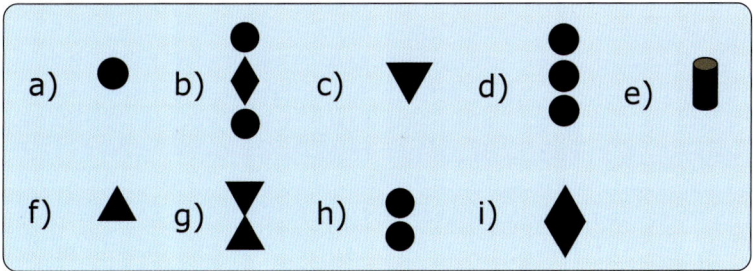

Fig 11.3 Day shapes.

11.9

What are the meanings of the sound signals in Fig 11.4?

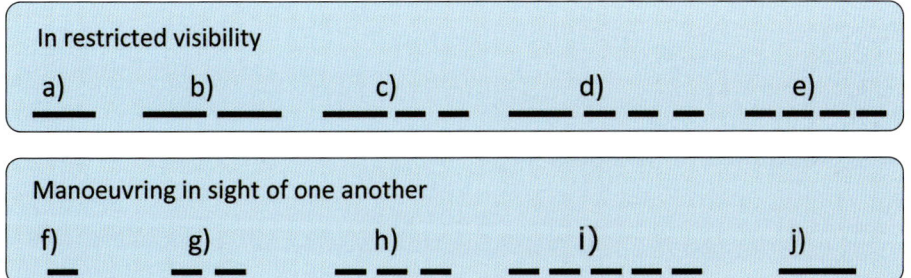

Fig 11.4 Sound signals.

11.10

What type of vessel is shown in each of the illustrations in Fig 11.5?

Mention its aspect, what length is indicated and whether it is underway, making way, or has stopped.

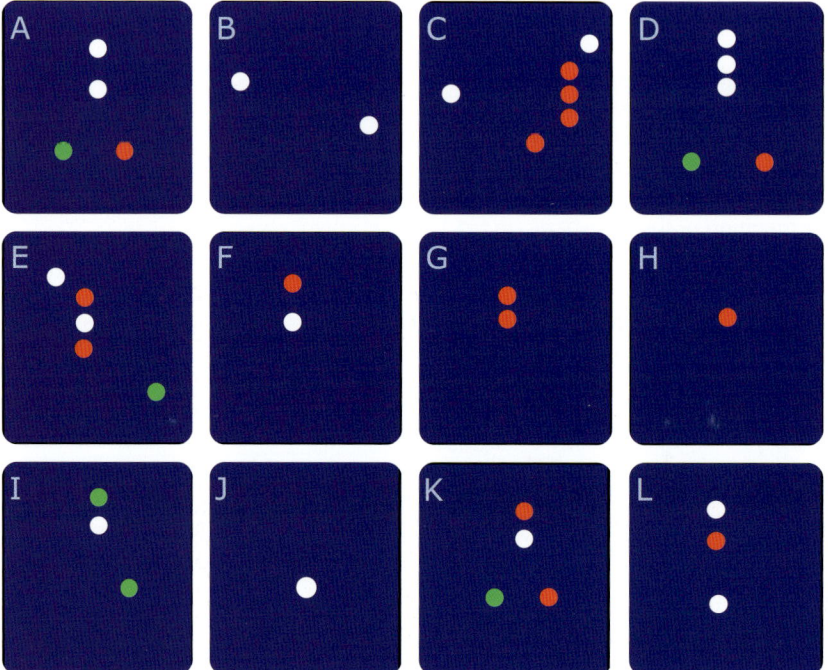

Fig 11.5 Navigation lights.

11.11

What lights should be shown by:

a) a 12-metre yacht when motor sailing?
b) a 15-knot, 8-metre semi-rigid inflatable?
c) a 6m semi-rigid inflatable with a maximum speed of 6 knots?
d) a 10-metre yacht under sail? Give two possible options.

11.12

According to the International Rules, by what methods could a 10-metre offshore yacht show that she is in distress? Give six examples.

12 METEOROLOGY

12.1

With reference to the shipping and other forecasts:

a) What height would the waves be when it is described as being *Moderate*?

b) What type of warning is issued if the wind is likely to be between 34 and 40 knots?

c) A *Strong Wind* warning is issued when the wind is forecast to reach which Beaufort force?

d) What would the visibility be if it was described as *Moderate*?

e) When would you expect a gale warning that has been forecast to arrive *Soon*?

f) When should a sea area be described as having *Wind cyclonic*?

12.2

Which of the following changes in barometric pressure are most likely to warn of strong to gale-force winds?

a) a fall of 3mb in the past 3 hours

b) a rise of 8mb in the past 3 hours

c) a fall of 8mb in the past 3 hours

12.3

You are in the English Channel steering a course of 270°T with the wind behind you.

Is the area of low pressure to the north or to the south of you?

12.4

What Beaufort wind force fits the following open sea conditions?

a) Large wavelets. Crests begin to break. Perhaps scattered white horses.

b) Moderate waves, taking more pronounced long form; many white horses are formed. Chance of some spray.

12.5

a) Which of the clouds shown in Fig 12.1 would be seen ahead of a warm front? A, B, C or D?

b) Which cloud would give heavy showers and gusty conditions? A, B, C, or D?

Fig 12.1 Cloud types.

12.6

Using the weather maps shown in Figure 12.2, estimate the wind direction and strength (light, moderate or strong) in each of the positions marked with an x.

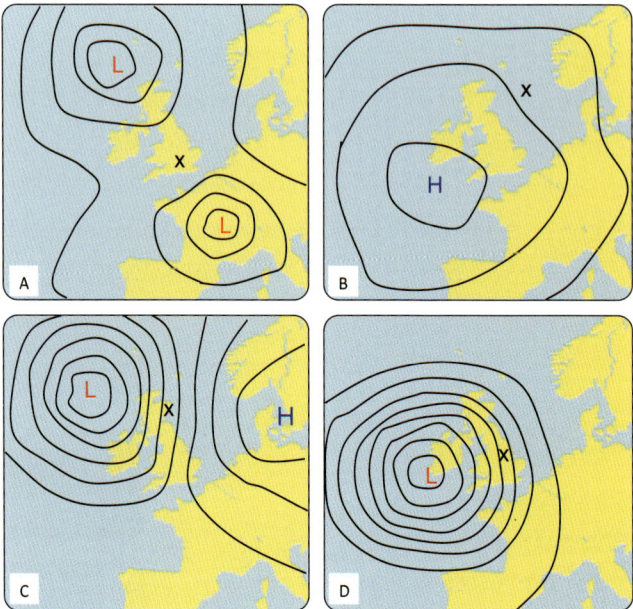

Fig 12.2 Weather maps.

12.7

Sea fog

a) What conditions are necessary for the formation of sea (advection) fog?
b) At what time of year is it most prevalent in the English Channel?
c) What conditions are necessary for its dispersal?
d) Why does it frequently form around headlands?

Radiation fog

e) At what times of the year does radiation fog form?
f) Will radiation fog burn off with the sun? Give reasons.

12.8

Use the weather chart in Figure 12.3 to answer the following questions:

a) What will be the wind direction on the western side of sea area Forties?
b) What weather feature lies in North Rockall?
c) What weather feature is coloured in purple?
d) Will the barometric pressure be rising or falling in sea area Fair Isle?

EXERCISES • METEOROLOGY

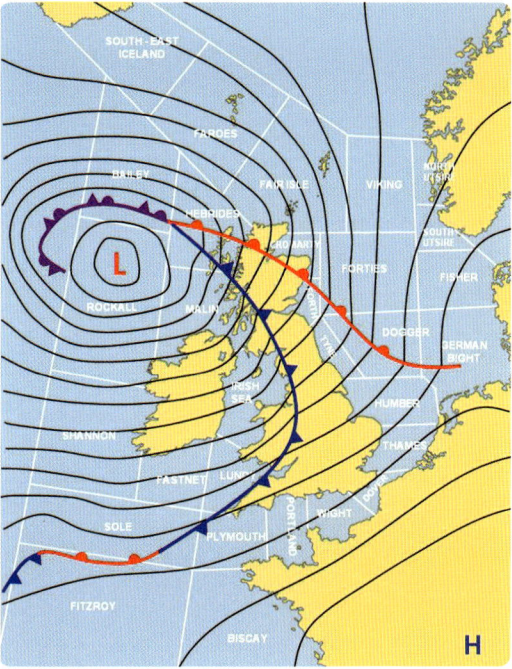

Fig 12.3 Synoptic chart with depression centred on sea area Rockall.

e) Will the visibility in sea area Tyne be good or poor?

f) Will the visibility in Fastnet be good or poor?

g) What cloud type would you expect in sea area Cromarty?

h) What type of front is depicted in blue?

i) Explain what is happening to the fronts in north Fitzroy.

12.9

It is June and a large area of high pressure is centred over the UK. The forecast is for light and variable winds and sea breezes along the coast.

a) Draw a diagram to show how the sea breeze forms.

b) Will the wind tend to back or veer during the day?

c) At what time of day will the breeze be strongest?

d) What will conditions be like during the evening?

12.10

Prior to your passage you will study your favourite weather sources, apps, or GRIB files.

a) What in basic terms should you check when comparing multiple sources?

b) After comparing the predictions how might you determine their accuracy?

13 SAFETY AND COMMUNICATIONS

13.1

The motor cruiser *Sinking Feeling* has been holed after hitting an underwater object and is taking on water faster than it can be pumped out. After making sure that all three crew are safe, have donned lifejackets, and are preparing the liferaft for launch, the skipper then goes to the VHF DSC radio to send a distress alert and message. The position is given as 50°10'.4N 001°18'.6W (south of the Isle of Wight). The MMSI is 235899983 and the callsign is 2ZXY.

a) Describe the actions needed in order to send a DSC distress alert.

b) What information is sent digitally when a DSC distress alert is made?

c) Does the shore station acknowledge your alert:
   i) by voice only?
   ii) digitally only?
   iii) both digitally and by voice?

d) Having sent the digital alert, how long should the skipper wait before sending the voice Mayday?

e) Write down the full voice distress message you would send.

13.2

A Search and Rescue helicopter is despatched to the stricken motor cruiser *Sinking Feeling*, which is now wallowing low in the water without any motive power.

a) Does the HM Coastguard helicopter approach on the port or starboard side of the craft?

b) What information is likely to be included in the briefing given on the VHF radio?

c) What type of flare might the crew be asked to use to pinpoint the boat's position?

d) Which type of flare should you definitely NOT use in close proximity of the helicopter?

Fig 13.1 *Sinking Feeling*.

13.3

Which VHF channel:

a) is the distress working and calling channel?

b) has been set aside for matters relating to navigational safety?

c) is used by HM Coastguard for small craft safety messages in the UK?

d) is used to call the majority of marinas in the UK?

Fig 13.2 Standard Horizon Matrix AIS/DSC VHF DSC.

13.4

a) What type of information is given by the Coastguard during their regular Maritime Safety Information broadcasts?

b) Are these broadcasts made:
   i) hourly?
   ii) three hourly?
   iii) four hourly?

13.5

You are viewing a sailing yacht with a regard to buying it, and the owner says that:

a) it has a high AVS. Explain what he means by this statement.

b) it is equipped with a 406MHz EPIRB. What is this and what would you have to do if you took over ownership of the vessel and the EPIRB?

b) What are the advantages of a modern 406MHz EPIRB with AIS?

13.6

A boat is equipped with an offshore flare pack. Which of the three flares in the photo would be most suitable for:

a) signalling distress when 10M offshore?

b) daytime use in bright sunshine and light winds for pinpointing the casualty's position in a distress situation?

c) pinpointing the position of a distressed craft within 3M of the shore?

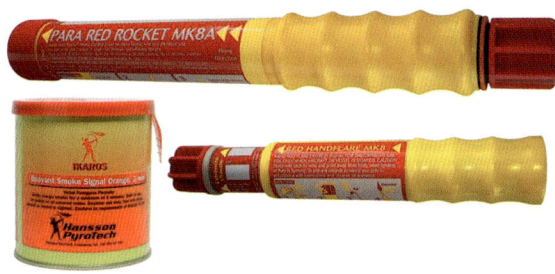

Fig 13.3 Types of flare.

YACHTMASTER EXERCISES FOR SAIL & POWER

13.7

If you had just purchased a brand-new flare pack, how long would it be before you needed to renew it?

13.8

You are entering an unfamiliar harbour at night. In the gloom you see that someone on a boat in the harbour is using a torch to flash two white, short flashes and a long flash in your direction.

a) What does this mean?

b) What should you now do?

13.9

A skipper is assisting the rescue services with a casualty at sea and has been communicating with a searching aircraft using the internationally recognised distress and life-saving signals that all craft are directed to carry. The aircraft passes low across his stern and rocks his wings. What is the aircraft telling the skipper?

Passage planning.

14 PLANNING AND MAKING PASSAGES

Use Stanfords Channel Island chart and 3°W variation. All times are given in BST and answers should be in BST. Use the extracts at the back of the book for port information.

Remember that International SOLAS rules legally require that a passage plan is made and that the following points (as a minimum) should be considered:

- Weather
- Tidal height/stream
- Navigation hazards
- Crew ability
- Condition of vessel

14

Most passage planning used to start with an idea in the pub or these days a coffee shop. Whether it's a day trip or an ocean crossing preparation is essential. What are the four key stages of passage planning?

14.1

Use Fig 14.1 and the extracts to answer the following questions:

a) What is the time of the morning HW at St Helier? Is it neaps, springs or mid range?

b) Between which times is there access to St Helier Marina?

c) Is there anywhere to wait in the port area if the marina is closed?

d) You decide that the route around Corbière Point will be the less stressful route. What is the approximate distance and passage time to Diélette's entrance?

e) At what time is HW Dover?

f) Between which times is the tidal stream favourable for the passage?

g) Is access to Diélette's outer harbour restricted in any way?

h) Use the tide difference on Dover (Diélette extracts) to determine between which times there is access to Diélette Marina during the middle of the day.

i) What dangers could be encountered en route?

j) At what time will you leave St Helier?

k) How can the skipper get information about wind strength outside the harbour?

	PASSAGE 1
Date	Sunday 5 September.
Passage	St Helier to Diélette Marina.
Boat	A 12-metre twin screw motor yacht with a draught of 1.2m. It cruises at 25 knots in a smooth sea but at 8 knots when the seas are choppy.
Present position	St Helier Marina.
Jersey C/G forecast	Light south-easterly at first with onshore sea breezes during the afternoon.
Crew	You as skipper with your wife and two teenagers. All know the boat.

Fig 14.1 Passage from St Helier to Diélette Marina.

YACHTMASTER EXERCISES FOR SAIL & POWER

Hard at chartwork.

14.2

Now that the basic planning has been done, you decide to enter a route into the GPS using the following waypoints:

1	49°09'.6N	002°10'.0W	Approx 2 cables south of Noirmont Point
2	49°10'.4N	002°17'.3W	Corbière Lighthouse bears 073°T 1.6M
3	49°14'.3N	002°18'.0W	Grosnez Point lighthouse bears 060°T 2.5M
4	49°18'.5N	002°14'.2W	Depth 19.8m (reduced to datum)
5	49°33'.0N	001°54'.5W	0.5M NW of West Cardinal Mark off Cap de Flamanville
6	49°33'.5N	001°52'.2W	0.5M NW of Diélette breakwater light

Enter the waypoints on the chart. List the true bearings and distances between each.

14.3

At 1300, you are cruising at 24kn when you fix the boat's position with reference to the centre of the compass rose to the west of Diélette. The given position is: 345°T to the waypoint 5.1M. The log reads 86.1.

a) Plot the position at 1300 and give the latitude and longitude.

b) Using the tidal stream charts and the deviation card in the extracts section, what is the compass course to steer to waypoint 5?

c) At what time will you get to waypoint 5?

14.4

As you approach the harbour your propeller hits something in the water and appears to suffer some damage. Does the harbour have facilities for lifting boats?

14.5

Use Fig 14.2 and extract 13 to answer the questions below:

HW St Peter Port 0905 BST 9.2m.

a) Between which times during the morning could the yacht leave Victoria Marina with 0.5m under the keel?

b) Where may visitors berth in the outer harbour?

	PASSAGE 2
Date	Wednesday 4 August.
Passage	St Peter Port, Guernsey to Granville on the Cherbourg Peninsula.
Boat	An 11-metre sailing yacht with 1.9m draught and an average cruising speed of 6 knots.
Present position	Victoria Marina at St Peter Port.
Shipping forecast	S or SE 4 or 5 veering W later and decreasing 3 or 4. Rain then at 0048 BST showers. Moderate becoming good.
Crew	Four in total – the skipper is an experienced offshore sailor.

Fig 14.2 Passage from Guernsey to Granville.

14.6

a) What is the approximate distance from St Peter Port entrance to the south-west corner of Jersey, and from there to Granville using the most direct route?

b) Roughly how long will it take to reach south-west Jersey? And how long from there to Granville (excluding any tidal advantage)?

14.7

a) Looking at the extracts for Granville, what is the time of HW at the relevant standard port during the evening of 4 August?

b) What is the time difference between the standard port HW and HW Granville?

c) Between which times during the evening is there access to Granville Marina?

d) What is the time of HW Dover on the afternoon of 4 August? Is it neaps or springs?

e) Looking at the tidal stream charts, what would be the best time to arrive at Granville during the evening?

14.8

a) At what time would you exit the marina at St Peter Port?

b) At what time would you leave St Peter Port for Granville?

14.9

Look back to the shipping forecast for 4 August (see Fig 14.2). What weather feature is due to pass over the area in the forecast period?

ON PASSAGE

Use 3°W variation and the deviation card at the back of the book.

14.10

The boat leaves the harbour at 1230 in the rain with moderate visibility and a fresh S wind. All the crew are looking forward to a bit of sunshine later on. The engine is switched off at 1300 when the Lower Heads Buoy is close to port. The skipper logs the position, zeros the log, and the boat sets off towards Jersey under reduced sail. It is estimated that, being well-heeled, the boat will make 10° leeway.

At 1400, in heavy rain and poor visibility, the skipper works up the estimated position to confirm the GPS fix. He records the information in Fig 14.3 in the logbook.

Time	Course	Log	Wind	L/Way	Baro	Depth	Notes
1300	135°C	0.0	S5	10°	1015	48m	At Lower Heads Buoy
1400	135°C	6.2	S5	10°	1014	50m	On S/B tack. EP using ◇J◇ HW St Helier 0958BST Sp. GPS 49°22'.5N 02°22'.4W

Fig 14.3 Logbook extract.

a) Plot the estimated position at 1400 BST.

b) The GPS position differs from the one worked out for the EP. Give reasons why this may have happened.

14.11

At 1900 the boat is 2.0M due east of Les Ardentes East Cardinal Mark, logging 7kn in a moderate westerly wind. The log reads 41.4.

a) Calculate the compass course to steer to a point midway between Anvers East Cardinal Mark and Basse du Founet Beacon. Use the heavily printed arrow and accompanying rates when plotting this tidal stream. There is no leeway.

b) What is the SOG?

14.12

a) As the boat approaches Granville, the skipper checks his pilot book. What dangers are there in the vicinity of the port?

b) How can the skipper quickly check that his depth calculations are correct?

15 CHARTWORK TEST PAPER 1

Use variation 3°W. Use the extracts section at the back of the book where necessary. Time zones vary from question to question.

15.1

When just south of Alderney, a navigator takes the following bearings at 1010 UTC on Tuesday 2 November. The log reads 20.6.

Quénard Point Headland	006°M
Water tower	321°M
The Noire Putes (northern rock)	287°M

Plot the 1010 fix and give the latitude and longitude.

15.2

From the 1010 UTC position, the navigator calculates the course to steer to a GPS waypoint off Cap de la Hague at 49°44′.4N 01°58′.4W using tidal diamond ⟨B⟩.

a) If the boat speed is 7kn, what answer does the navigator get?

b) At what time (UTC) during the afternoon does the tidal stream become unfavourable around Cap de la Hague?

15.3

The log extract in Fig 15.1 is from a yacht on passage from Alderney to Guernsey.

Plot the estimated positions at 0800 BST and at 0900 BST.

15.4

Tidal information for Barfleur is shown at the bottom of page 103.

At 1055 (FSumT) on Saturday 25 September, a yacht with a draught of 1.8m prepares to anchor off Barfleur.

a) What are the heights and times (FSumT) of HW and LW in Barfleur during the day?

b) What is the height of tide at 1055 FSumT?

c) In what depth of water should the skipper anchor so that there is a 1.0m clearance at LW?

Thursday 21 October. Time Zone BST

Time	Co°C	Log	Wind	L/Way	Baro	Depth	Notes
0700	270	22.1	SW4/5	10°	1005	47.2m	Position: 49°36′.2N 02°22′.0W
0800	270	26.6	SW4	10°	1004	53.6m	Tacked onto 170°C. EP using ⟨C⟩
0900	170	30.7	SW3	10°	1004	10.1m	EP plotted using ⟨C⟩

Fig 15.1 Logbook extract.

16 CHARTWORK TEST PAPER 2

Use variation 3°W. Time zones vary from question to question. Use the extracts section at the back of the book where necessary.

16.1

At 1450 BST on Sunday 12 September, the following bearings were taken by the skipper of a motor cruiser off the north coast of Jersey. Plot the fix and give the latitude and longitude.

Western radio mast at Bouley Bay	161°M
TV mast	218°M
Sorel Point lighthouse	256°M

16.2

From the position of the 1450 BST fix, the skipper of the cruiser weighs anchor and steers a course of 023°C at 12kn en route for Diélette.

a) Plot the estimated position at 1520 using tidal diamond ⟨K⟩.

b) How far will the boat be from Les Dirouilles rocks at the closest point?

c) At what time (BST) will the cruiser be closest to the rocky patch?

d) What other method could the skipper have used to ensure that the boat remained at least 1M to the west of Les Dirouilles rocks?

16.3

On Thursday 14 October, a yacht on passage from Diélette to Jersey is sailing on a fine reach in a SE wind. It is estimated that the yacht is making 5° leeway in a short choppy sea.

At 1420 BST, the navigator fixes position by GPS 222°T 3.6M using a waypoint at Plateau des Trois-Grunes West Cardinal Mark (north of Les Écréhou).

Use the tidal stream charts to determine the magnetic course to steer to a point 1.0M east of Écrevière South Cardinal Mark. The speed through the water is 4kn.

16.4

On Sunday 14 November, a skipper intends to dry his boat out in St Catherine's Bay on the east coast of Jersey in order to effect some underwater repairs. His boat draws 1.4m and he anchors in 3.0m of water at 0925 UTC.

a) At what time (UTC) will the boat ground?

b) At what time (UTC) will the boat dry out?

c) At what time (UTC) will it refloat?

ANSWERS

1 CHARTS

1.1
Admiralty chart booklet 5011.

1.2
Charted depth will be 10m or more.

1.3
a) Overfalls or tide rip.

b) Tidal diamond A.

c) The nature of the seabed is predominantly rock but also has some broken shells.

d) Marina or yacht harbour.

Steer 105 degrees, skipper!

37

1.4

Grand Léjon lighthouse.

Light = red and white sectored light that flashes 5 times within a 20-second period.

Nominal range = 18 nautical miles for the white light and 14 nautical miles for the red.

Height of light = 17 metres above mean high water springs.

1.5

a) European Datum (1950).

b) WGS84.

1.6

A rhumb line.

1.7

a) Rock, depth unknown, considered to be dangerous to surface navigation.

b) A non-dangerous wreck. (In over 200m or depth unknown, which is not considered dangerous to surface navigation.)

c) A rock which covers and uncovers. Height above datum 3.6 metres.

d) Wreck showing any part of hull or superstructure at the level of chart datum.

e) Rock that covers and uncovers. Height 4.2m above chart datum.

f) Dangerous wreck over which the depth of 3.2m has been obtained by sounding, not wire sweep.

g) Rock awash at the level of chart datum.

h) Wreck, depth unknown, which is considered potentially dangerous to surface navigation.

1.8

Vector charts.

1.9

Raster charts are just a copy of the original paper chart. Zooming in does not reveal any further detail.

Vector charts use a bank of data with more and more information being revealed as the scale is increased with zooming. Details may be included or omitted on demand. This type of chart is favoured by the maritime organisation controlling merchant shipping.

2 COMPASS

ANSWERS

2.1

The variation in 2019 is 3°20'W and it is forecast to decrease by 8 minutes each year.

The variation in 2024 will therefore be 40 minutes less than in 2019.

The variation in 2024 will be 2°40'W. For navigational purposes this would be rounded up to 3°W.

2.2

Deviation is an error that occurs when the boat's magnetic field affects the compass reading. Deviation can be caused by:

a) Ferrous objects, such as the engine, iron keel, handheld flares and tool kits.

b) The electromagnetic effect from mobile phones, cables carrying electrical current and radio transmissions.

c) The magnetic influence from some large outboard motors, loudspeakers and analogue navigation instruments.

2.3

Yes, electronic (fluxgate) compasses suffer from deviation but, if set up correctly, are usually self-adjusting.

2.4

No, the yacht's compass will probably be insufficiently damped for your speedboat. The compass card may well behave erratically – or even spin.

Fig A2.1 Raymarine electronic compass.

2.5

Looking at the chart a note is placed close to Grand Léjon that states:

'*Local Magnetic Anomalies (see Note)*'.

This means that any compass bearing taken in the vicinity is likely to be inaccurate. The GPS would not be thus affected as magnetism is not used to fix the position.

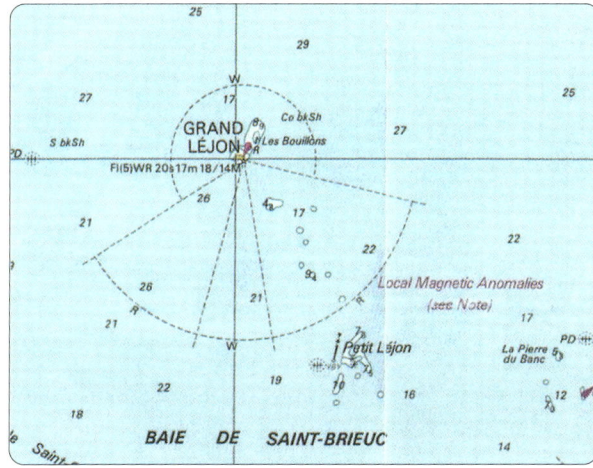

Fig A2.2 Magnetic anomalies off the French coast.

2.6

a) 065°T + 5°W   = 070°M
b) 005°T − 8°E   = 357°M
c) 247°T − 15°E   = 232°M
d) 357°T + 4°W   = 001°M

2.7

a) 135°M − 12°W   = 123°T
b) 315°M + 10°E   = 325°T
c) 002°M − 3°W   = 359°T
d) 180°M + 6°E   = 186°T

2.8

a) 180°C +2°E Dev   = 182°M − 3°W Var = 179°T
b) 146°C No Dev   = 146°M − 3°W Var = 143°T
c) 225°C +3°E Dev   = 228°M − 3°W Var = 225°T
d) 338°C −1°W Dev   = 337°M − 3°W Var = 334°T

2.9

Leading lights are on a bearing of 023°T

Variation   +3°W
Compass should read   026°M
Compass actually reads   023°C
Deviation is   3°E

The rhyme 'If error is East then the compass will read least' works well here.

2.10

Transit = 308°T + 3°W Variation = 311°M.

Compass reads 309°C (compass least – error east) so the deviation is 2°E.

2.11

Calibration is required to compensate for any ferrous or electromagnetic influences from the boat. The manufacturer will explain the process in his instructions but in outline it requires the vessel to be driven round a circular path twice at a given speed over a given time. This will allow the compass to work out the deviation and make corrections for it. A very similar method is used for calibrating mobile phones and tablets.

ANSWERS

3 POSITION FIXING

3.1

See plot (Fig A3.1). Position at 1000: 49°12′.3W 002°17′.6W.

3.2

See plot (Fig A3.1). Approximate position at 1630 is over Rigdon Bank.

The two position lines give a narrow cut but depths are always a good check. The distance from the shore should make this an adequate fix, although the bearings were taken quickly.

Fig A3.1 Q 3.1, 3.2, 3.3, 3.4.

YACHTMASTER EXERCISES FOR SAIL & POWER

3.3

See plot (Fig A3.1). Position at 1500: Noirmont Point 218°T 3.0M.

3.4

See plot (Fig A3.1) Position at 1800: 49°09′.3N 002°17′.6W.

3.5

See plot (Fig A3.2). The fix lies very close to the 10m contour.

3.6

See plot (Fig A3.2). The area of uncertainty is over half a square mile but is better than no fix at all. Provided that there is sufficient depth of water, it should be safe to proceed as the run into Granville is reasonably straightforward, although the depths are very varied. Point du Roc Lighthouse has a distinctive fog horn and a powerful light, which should be seen through the mist at a safe distance. The fog may well thin over the shallower water as the coast is closed.

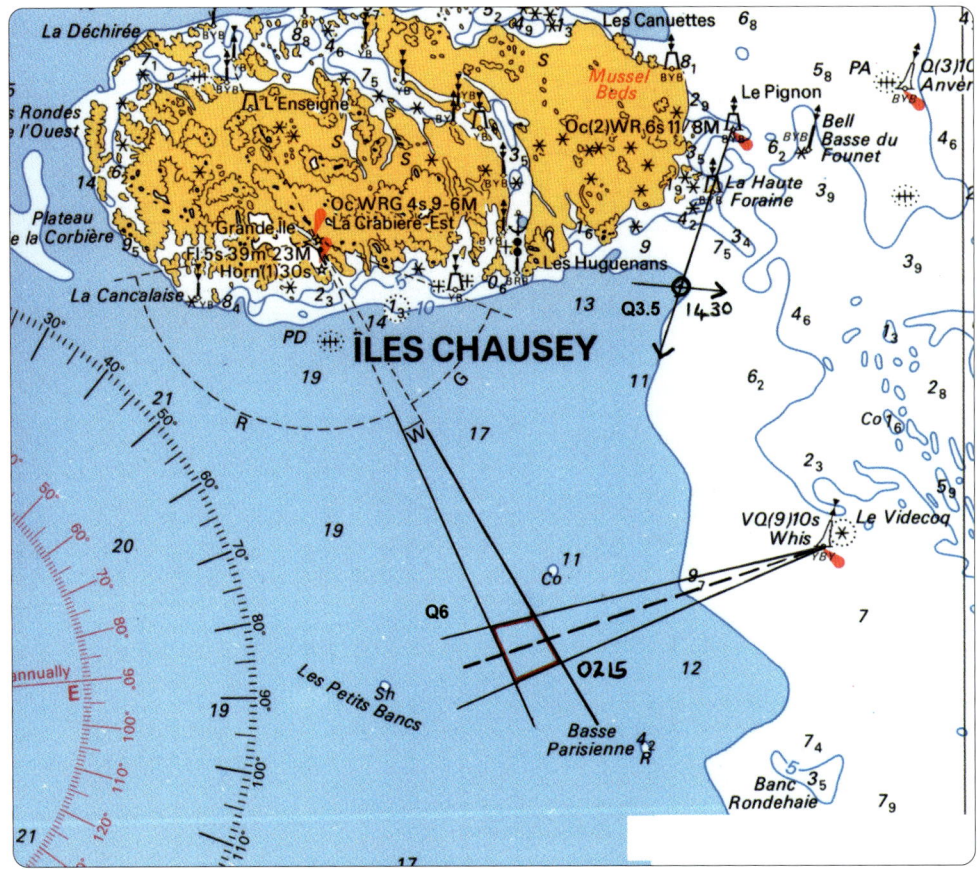

Fig A3.2 Q3.5 & 3.6

4 BUOYS, LIGHTS AND LIGHTHOUSES

ANSWERS

4.1

a) IALA system A is used in Europe and much of the world and IALA system B is used in the Americas and Pacific rim countries.

b) The colour of the lateral buoys is the only difference between the two systems. The colour is reversed but the shape remains the same. IALA A uses the colour GREEN for the conical buoys and RED for the can-shaped ones.

IALA B uses the colour RED for the conical buoys and GREEN for the can-shaped buoys (as shown in the Hudson River in Fig A4.1).

Fig A4.1 A port-hand mark off New York.

4.2

a) A north cardinal beacon – pass to the north.

b) La Horaine. Lighted beacon, group flash 3 every 12s, 13m above MHWS with a luminous range of 11M. (Not to be confused with an east cardinal mark.)

4.3

A An isolated danger mark. Pass either side.

The light is WHITE flashing in groups of two.

B A safe water mark, sometimes called a fairway buoy. Pass either side. It is usually placed as the first buoy when entering a harbour before a line of lateral marks.

The light is WHITE and will be either long flashing, isophase, occulting or morse A.

C A special mark. It can be used for racing marks and large ship mooring buoys, to show water skiing areas and to mark gunnery ranges.

The light is YELLOW and uses a sequence not used for a white light. It therefore mostly flashes in groups of four.

4.4

A *flashing* light is off for longer than it is on.

An *occulting* light is on for longer than it is off.

An *isophase* light has equal periods of light and dark.

4.5

a) See Fig A4.3. The post that is predominantly red with a narrow green band as it is the port-hand mark for the major channel and the starboard-hand mark for the minor channel.

b) A red light.

c) Flashing 2 + 1.

4.6

a) The leading lights for St Malo have a fixed green light (ie they show a continuous light).

b) Yes. The lights have a nominal range of 22M and 25M so would be seen easily.

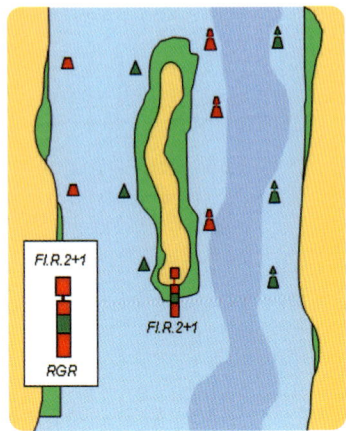

Fig A4.3 Preferred channel.

4.7

The position is in:

a) the RED sector of Grand Léjon light.

b) the GREEN sector of Rohein.

c) the WHITE sector of Erquy light.

4.8

Point Corbière Lighthouse has:

- An isophase light (equal periods of light and dark) with white and red sectors and a 10-second sequence.
- The centre of the light is 36m above MHWS.
- The nominal ranges of the white and red light are 18M and 16M respectively.
- The foghorn sounds with a letter C in Morse code, ie long, short, long, short, every 60 seconds.

4.9

AIS can be added to existing navigation marks, making them easier to locate at a greater distance or in reduced visibility.

- Virtual AIS buoys can be placed quickly to mark a new wreck or obstruction (isolated danger), in areas where it is impossible to place a physical aid to navigation, and where buoys are seasonally lifted due to ice.
- The disadvantage, as they are virtual, is that they do not exist and cannot be seen. Also only vessels with AIS fitted can find them.

ANSWERS

5 TIDAL HEIGHTS

5.1

i) A
ii) E
iii) L
iv) J
v) K
vi) C
vii) H
viii) F
ix) M
x) B
xi) G
xii) D

5.2

a) The charted depth is drying 4.5m, so the depth of water is 6.8m – 4.5m = 2.3m.

b) The charted depth is 4.4m, so the depth is 4.4m + 6.8m = 11.2m.

5.3

a) Les Bas-Sablons light is 20m above MHWS.
MHWS St Malo is 12.2m. MLWN St Malo is 4.2m. Height difference = 8.0m.
The height of the light above the water at MLWN = 28.0m.

b) Charted depth close to the ferry terminal is 1.6m. Height of MLWS = 1.5m.
The depth of water at MLWN is 1.6m + 1.5m = 3.1m.

c) Bridge clearance height is calculated above Highest Astronomical Tide (HAT).
HAT = 13.6m MHWS = 12.2. Difference = 1.4m.
Clearance above mast = 20.0m + 1.4m – 17.0m = 4.4m.

d) Draught of boat = 2.2m.
Depth of water at MHWN was 8.0m.
Clearance under the keel at MHWN was therefore 5.8m.
Fall of tide from MHWN to MLWN = 5.1m.
Clearance under the keel at MLWN = 0.7m.

5.4

When the pressure is high it is often during a period of calm winds so there should not be any large waves damaging shoreside installations. However, the tidal height will be lower than forecast as the high pressure air pushes the water levels downward. With pressures of 1040 to 1050 millibars the water could be approx 0.3m lower than forecast.

5.5

Saturday 4 September – St Helier:

HW St Helier is 0927 UT = 1027 BST.

HW = 10.00m LW 2.4m. Range is 7.6m = mid range.

Height of tide from graph = 5.8m.

YACHTMASTER EXERCISES FOR SAIL & POWER

5.6

Using the table in Extract 13 for St Peter Port, the earliest time there will be 2.1m over the sill is 2hrs before HW = 1344.

5.7

Saturday 5th June:

HW St Malo 0934 French Summer Time 12.1m LW 1.7m.

Height of tide required = 1.5m (clearance) + 1.5m (draught) + 1.1m (drying ht) = 4.1m.

The boat must leave by 1434.

5.8

Sunday 12th September:

Range 3.8m   Mid range

Cherbourg (FStanT)	LW 1415	2.0m	HW 1949	5.8m
St Vaast differences	+0117	−0.2m	+ 54	+0.3m
St Vaast FSumT	**1632**	**1.8m**	**2143**	**6.1m**

5.9

Thursday 9th December:

St Helier (UT)	LW 1017	2.9m	HW 1603	9.6m
Braye differences	+55	−1.1m	+48	−4.1m
Braye UT	**1112**	**1.8m**	**1651**	**5.5m**

5.10

Thursday 22nd July:

a)   Standard port for Diélette is St Malo.

St Malo FStanT	HW 1005	10.8m	LW 2.8m	HW 2215	11.0m	Mid range
Diélette differences	+39	−2.2m	−0.5m	+40	−2.25m	
Times FSumT	**1144**	**8.6m**	**2.3m**	**2355**	**8.75m**	

ANSWERS • TIDAL HEIGHTS

b) Boat grounds at 1545, which is HW + 4 hours.
Height of tide at 1545 = 4.9m.

Redo the plot using the next HW times and heights.
Remember to go halfway between the spring and neap curve as it is mid range.

c) The tide will rise to 4.9m at next HW – 3 hours 05 mins = 2049 approx.

5.11

Tuesday 15 June:

Range 7.1m / 7.4m Mid range

St Malo (FStanT)	1st HW	0526	10.3m	LW	3.2m	2nd HW	1745	10.6m
Chausey differences		+5	+0.7m		+0.5m		+5	+0.7m
Chausey (FSumT)		**0631**	**11.0m**		**3.7m**		**1850**	**11.3m**

a) From St Malo curve with Chausey data: Height of tide at 1000 = 7.5m

b) The tide has to drop to 1.0m for the boat to ground.
Boat will therefore ground when the height of tide = 6.5m at 1041 approx.

c) She will be completely dry when the height of tide = 5.0m at 1150 approx.

d) Using data for 2nd HW and calculating for mid range: the water will reach the keel again at 1450 approx.

Starboard-hand post with tide gauge.

This port-hand post should not be passed close to port!

6 TIDAL STREAMS

6.1

a) HW Dover −2hrs 330°T 0.7kn.

b) HW Dover +4hrs 143°T 5.2kn.

c) HW Dover −4hrs 085°T 2.6kn.

6.2

a) **7 September:**

HW Dover 0522 BST. Range 3.0m, neaps.
HW hour 0452–0552.
HW −2 0252–0352 265°T 1.4kn.

b) **16 October:**

HW Dover 1301 BST. Range 6.0m, springs.
HW hour 1231–1331.
HW −5 0731–0831 BST. 035°T 5.2kn.

c) **1 November:**

HW Dover 1314 UTC. Range 4.8m, mid range.
HW hour 1244–1344.
HW +5 1744–1844 130°T 3.0kn (by interpolation).

6.3

Using data for diamond ⟨L⟩ from tidal stream panel at bottom of chart:

a) St Helier +5hrs = 282°T 3.5kn.

b) St Helier −2hrs = 110°T 1.7kn.

c) St Helier −6hrs = 287°T 1.3kn.

6.4

Using tidal diamond ⟨E⟩:

a) **Thursday 16 September:**

St Helier HW 0828 BST. 10.9m LW 1.3m. Range 9.6m, springs.
HW hour = 0758 to 0858.
HW +2 = 0958 to 1058 = 033°T 3.3kn.

ANSWERS • TIDAL STREAMS

b) **Monday 8 November:**

St Helier HW 0258 UT. 8.1m LW 4.0m. Range 4.1m, neaps.
HW hour = 0228 to 0328.
HW +5 = 0728 to 0828 = 213°T 1.7kn.

c) **Tuesday 19th October:**

St Helier HW 2253 BST. 9.3m LW 2.7m. Range 6.6m, mid range.
HW hour = 2223 to 2323.
HW –4 = 1823 to 1923 = 213°T 1.95kn.

6.5

Saturday 25 September:

Dover HW 2218 BST.
HW hour 2148 to 2248.
Stream is slack HW –5 = 1648 to 1748.

6.6

1 October:

- Distance from Cherbourg to St Peter Port is approximately 40M, a passage of about 1½hrs (excluding tidal stream).
- HW Dover 1342 BST. Range 5.9m, springs. HW hour 1312–1412.

The sea will be calmest between HW –5 and HW –2 when the strongest stream is with the wind, and during the slack water period just after that. Even with the stream running strongly, the speed of the boat is sufficient to punch both the tidal stream and the wind. The passage can easily be completed between 0812 and 1112.

The key to success is to pass Cap de la Hague at slack water to avoid the strongest currents therefore a slightly earlier start (HW –6) could be considered as beneficial.

6.7

This is not a physical 'gate' in the true sense. It refers to the time when the tidal stream is favourable, ie the 'gate' is open. Cruising the Channel Islands successfully depends on getting the 'gate' times worked out as it is impossible to proceed against a spring stream of 7kn when your top speed is 6kn!

6.8

a) **True**. It is usually shallower inshore where the flow is slowed by surface friction.

b) **False**. At equinoctial springs the range can be far greater than the mean. For example, turn to the extract section and compare the range during the late evening of 29/30 September at St Helier with the mean range. The mean is 9.6m, but on that evening the actual range is 10.6m.

c) **True**. During the early afternoon of 30 September, HW Dover is at 1307 BST and it can be seen from the tidal stream atlas (extracts) that the stream turns from north-going to south-going off the eastern side of Guernsey at HW Dover −1 hr 30 mins at approx 1130. However, HW St Peter Port is at 0831 BST, which means that the stream outside St Peter Port entrance changes at local HW +3.

d) **True**. The Alderney Race has streams of up to 10kn at springs, and when this stream has strong winds blowing against it, the area becomes a maelstrom – not a pretty sight!

e) **False**.

f) **True**. Any prominent headland will cause the water to deviate around it. As the stream bends, it accelerates – as shown in the illustration of the notorious Portland Race (Fig A6.1).

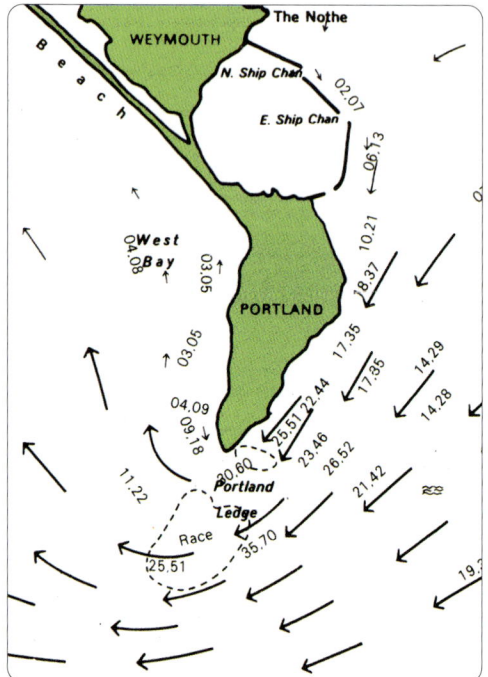

Fig A6.1 Portland tidal streams.

7 COURSE TO STEER

ANSWERS

7.1

See Fig A7.1.

CTS = 040°T + 3°W = 043°M.

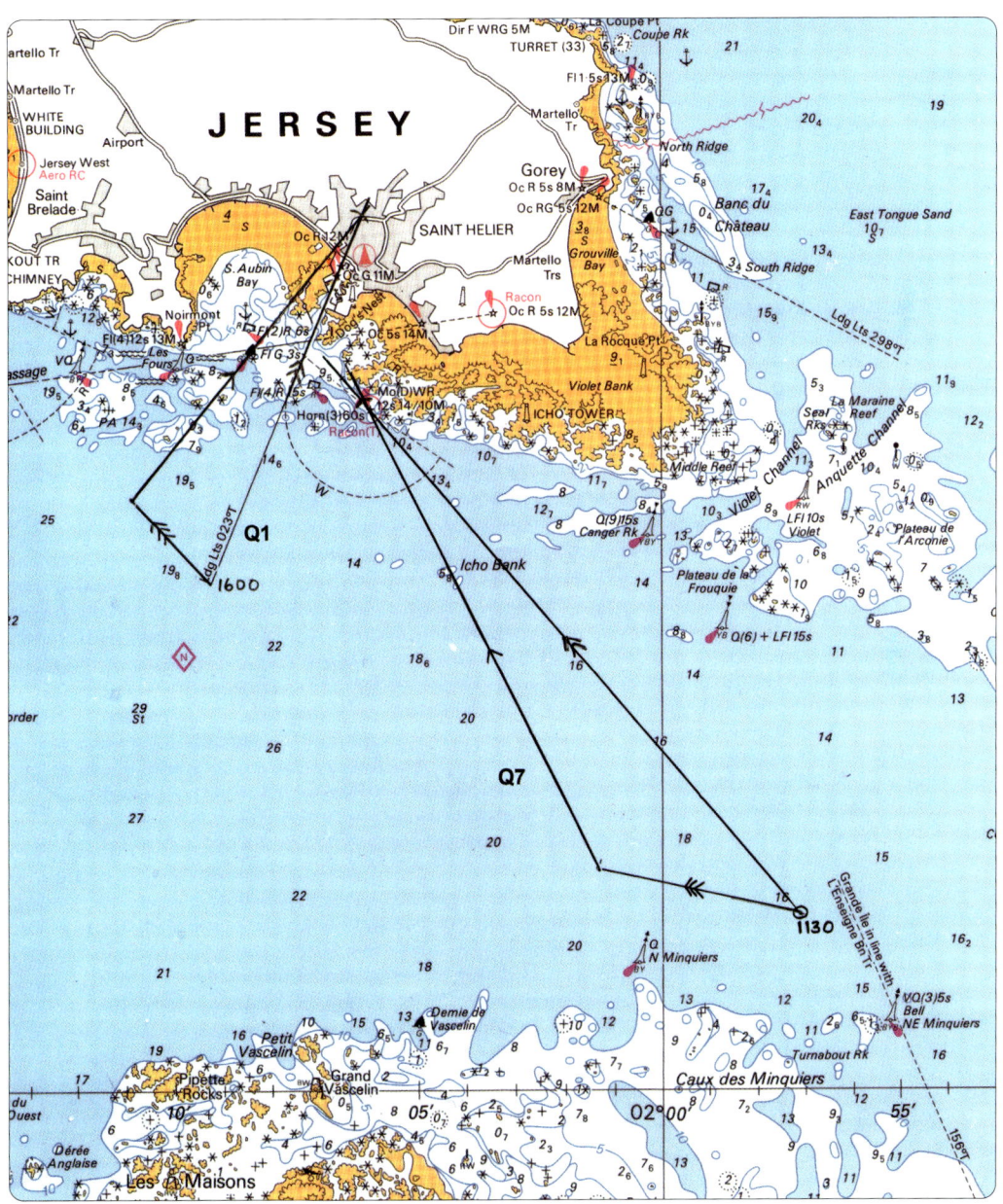

Fig A7.1 Q7.1 & 7.7.

YACHTMASTER EXERCISES FOR SAIL & POWER

7.2

A half-hour plot is best for this question.

a) CTS 192°T +3°W = 195°M

b) Calculating for time uses the formula:
$$\frac{\text{Distance to travel 9.0M}}{\text{Speed over ground 17.2kn}} \times 60 = \text{Passage time in minutes} = 31 \text{ minutes}$$

ETA at the buoy = 1831.

7.3

a) CTS 172°T + 3°W = 175°M

b) As the two tidal vectors are very similar, the bearing to the waypoint should be roughly the same as the course over ground. If it is not then some course adjustment would be necessary.

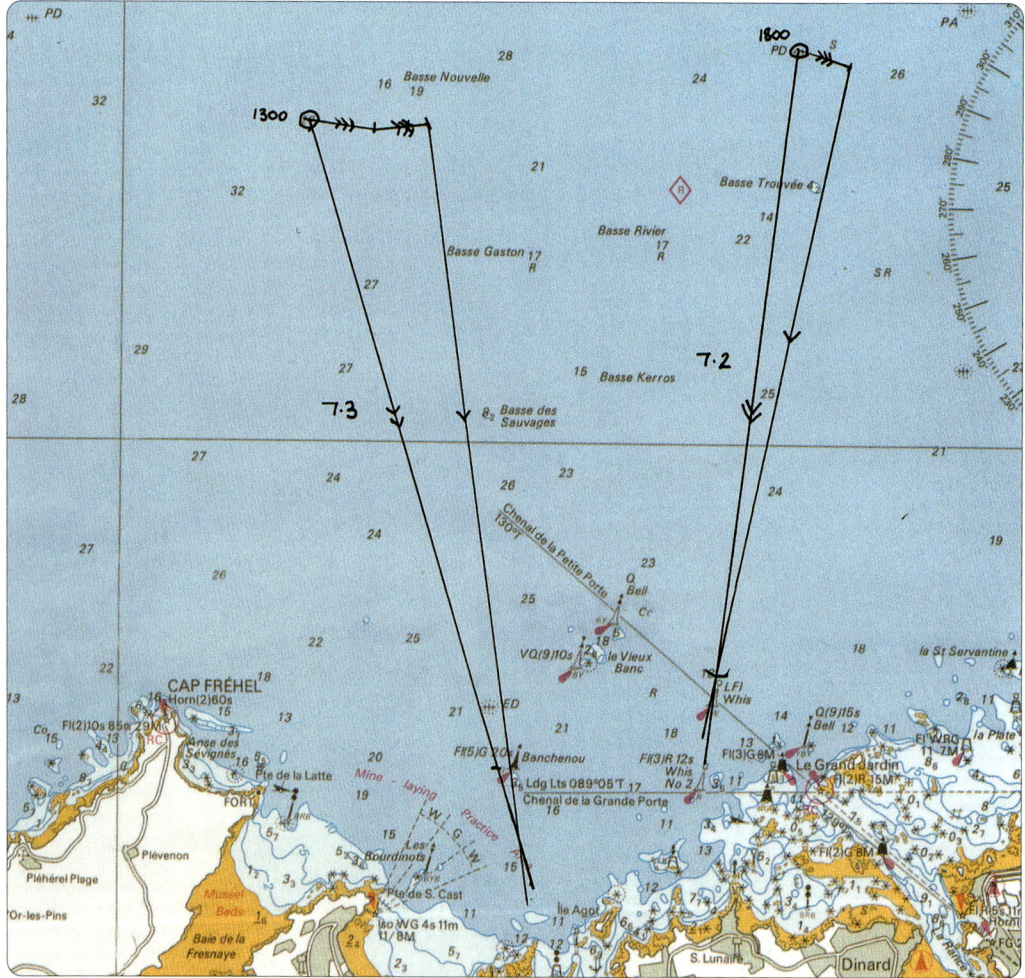

Fig A7.2 Q7.2 & 7.3.

ANSWERS • COURSE TO STEER

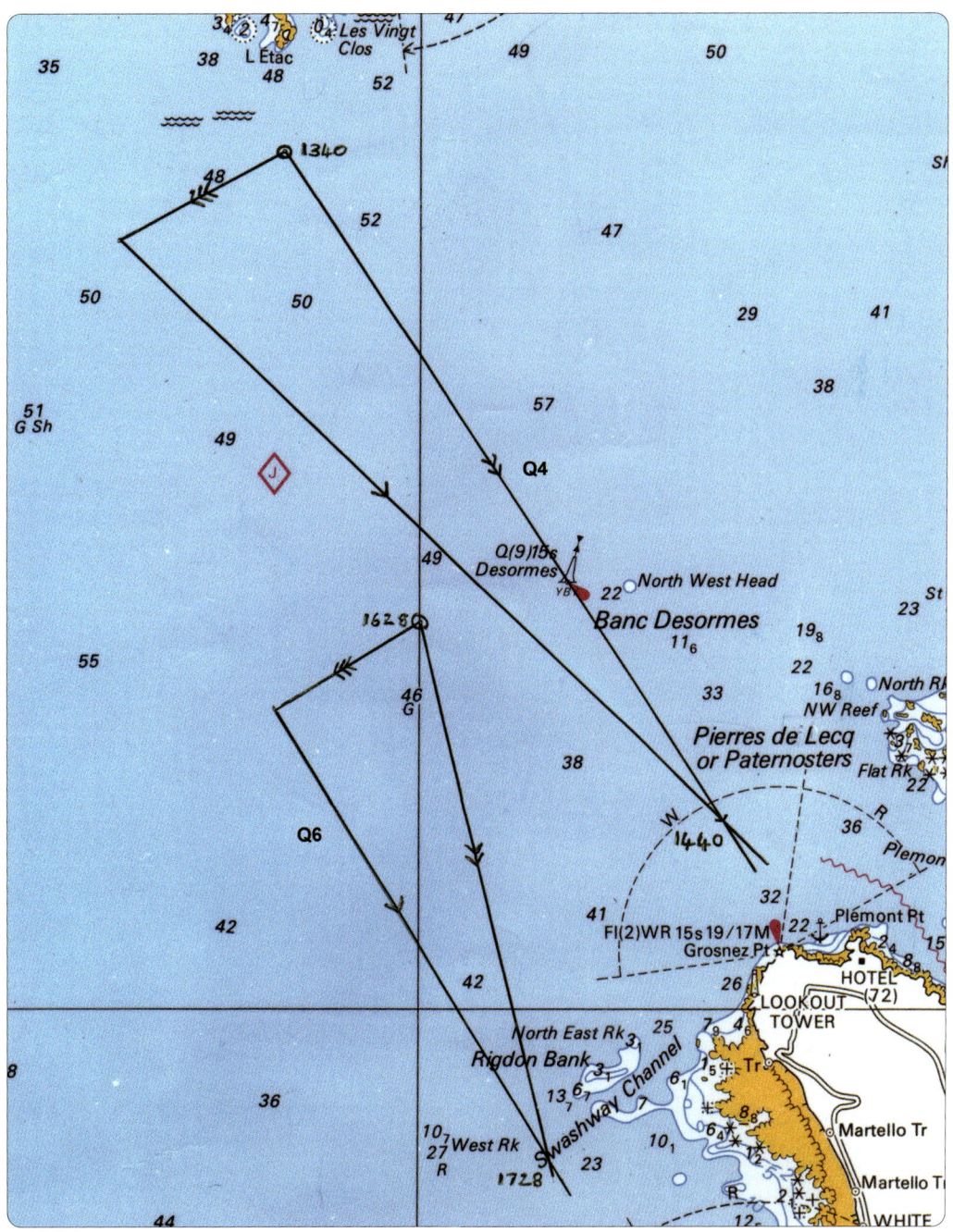

Fig A7.3 Q7.4 & 7.6.

7.4

See Fig A7.3.
17 October:

a) HW St Helier 0911 BST. Range 9.5m, springs.

b) HW hour = 0841–0941.

   HW +5hrs 1341–1441 242°T 1.8kn.

c) CTS = 134°T + 3°W = 137°M.

d) Distance to the buoy (4.9M) ÷ speed over ground (7.6kn) x 60 = 39 mins.
   Boat will reach the buoy at 1340 + 39 mins = 1419 BST.

7.5

See Fig A7.4.
28 October:

a) HW St Helier 1937 BST. Springs. Range is 9.5m – very close to the mean spring range.

b) 1407–1507 HW –5 = 232°T 2.6kn.

c) 349°T + 3°W = 352°M.

d) Just under half an hour.

7.6

See Fig A7.3.
5 September:

a) HW Dover 1558 BST. Range 4.5m, mid range.
   HW hour 1528–1628.
   HW +1hr 1628–1728 239°T. Spring 2.4kn. Neap 1.0kn. Mid 1.7kn.
   CTS = 148°T +3°W = 151°M.

b) To correct for 10° push to port, it will be necessary to alter 10° to starboard (into the wind) to stay on track.
   CTS with leeway = 151°M + 10° = 161°M.

7.7

See Fig A7.1.
17 September:

a) HW St Helier 0901 BST. Range 9.7m, springs.
   HW hour = 0831–0931.
   Time of passage = HW +3hrs = 1131–1231.
   ◇N 282°T 2.9kn.
   CTS = 333°T + Variation 3°W = 336°M + Deviation 2°W = 338°C.

ANSWERS • COURSE TO STEER

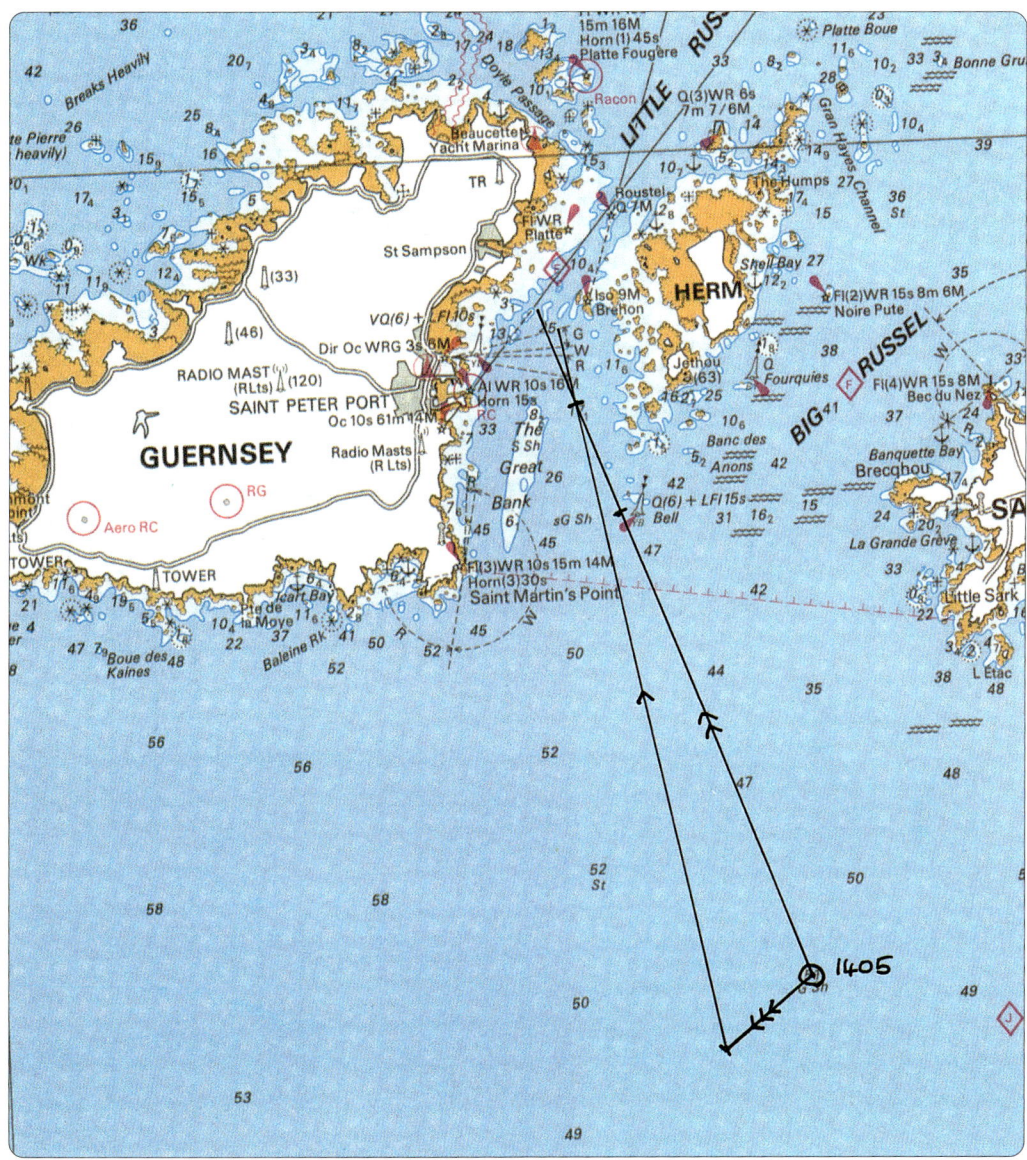

Fig A7.4 Q7.5.

b) COG = 319°T.
   SOG = 9.0kn.

c) Distance 8.8M ÷ SOG 9.0kn x 60 = 59 mins.
   ETA = 1130 + 59 mins = 1229 BST.

8 DEAD RECKONING AND ESTIMATED POSITION

8.1
There is a dangerous wreck that has a charted depth of 6.3m below chart datum.

8.2
a) 48°39′.1N 002°32′.3W.

b) 135°T.

c) 4kn.

8.3
See Fig A8.2. 325°T 2.35M

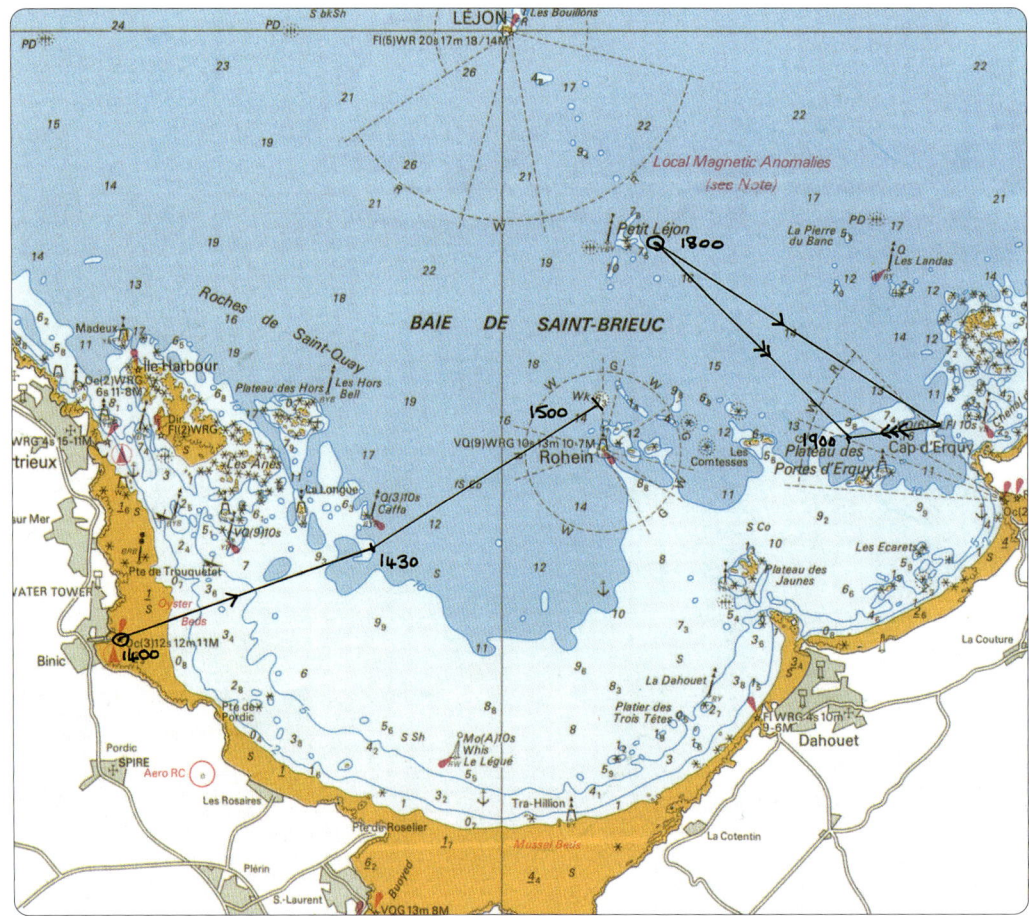

Fig A8.1 Q8.1 & 8.2.

ANSWERS • DEAD RECKONING AND ESTIMATED POSITION

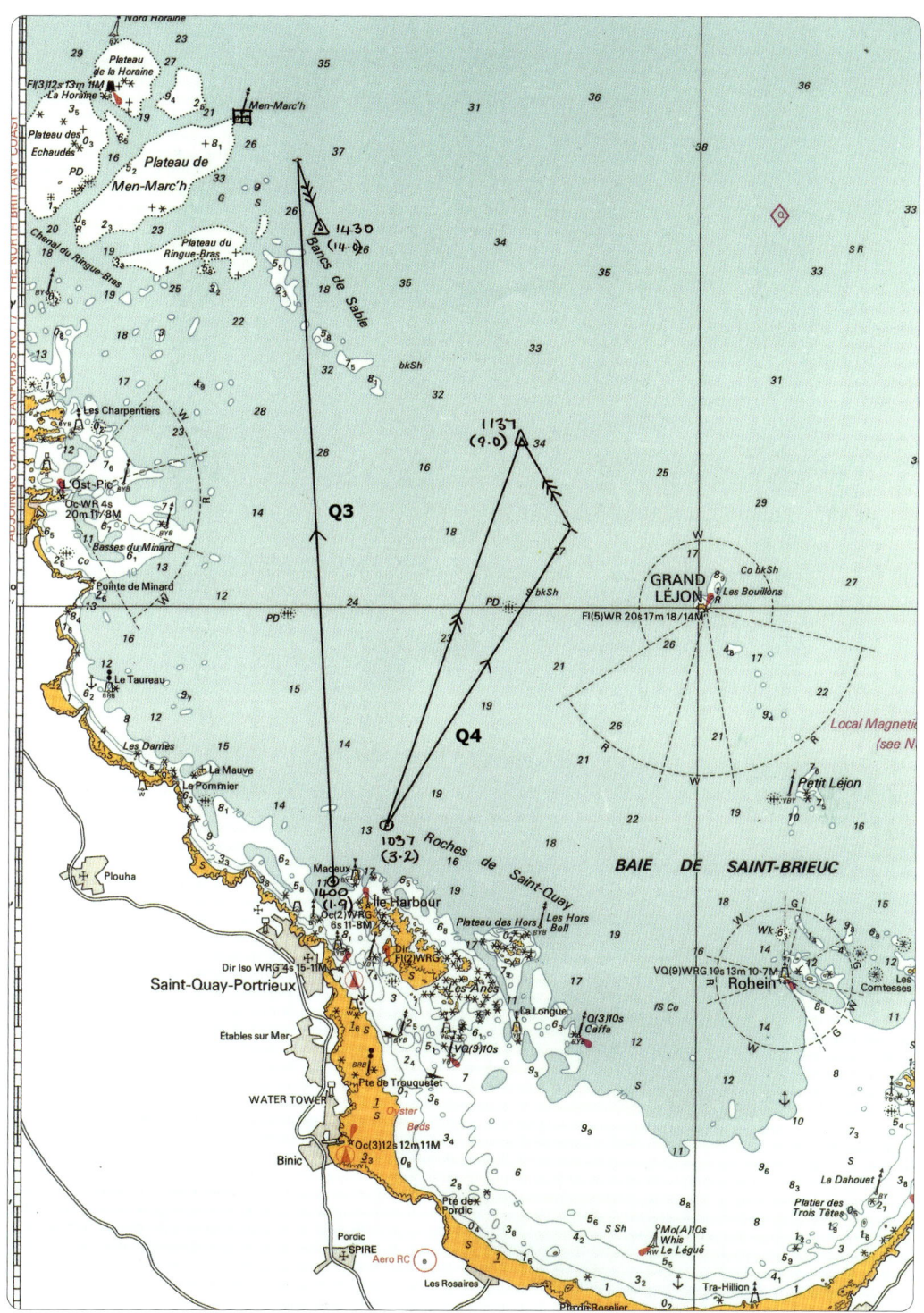

Fig A8.2 Q8.3 & 8.4.

YACHTMASTER EXERCISES FOR SAIL & POWER

8.4

See Fig A8.2.

30 September:

a) HW Dover 1307 BST. Range 6.1, springs.

b) HW hour 1237–1337. HW −2 = 1037–1137 = 330°T 1.7kn.

c) EP 48°47'.7N 002°44'.4W.

d) COG = 019°T. SOG = 6.8kn.

8.5

See Fig A8.3.

a) 49°06'.7N 002°51'.0W.

b) No, the yacht will not clear the area.

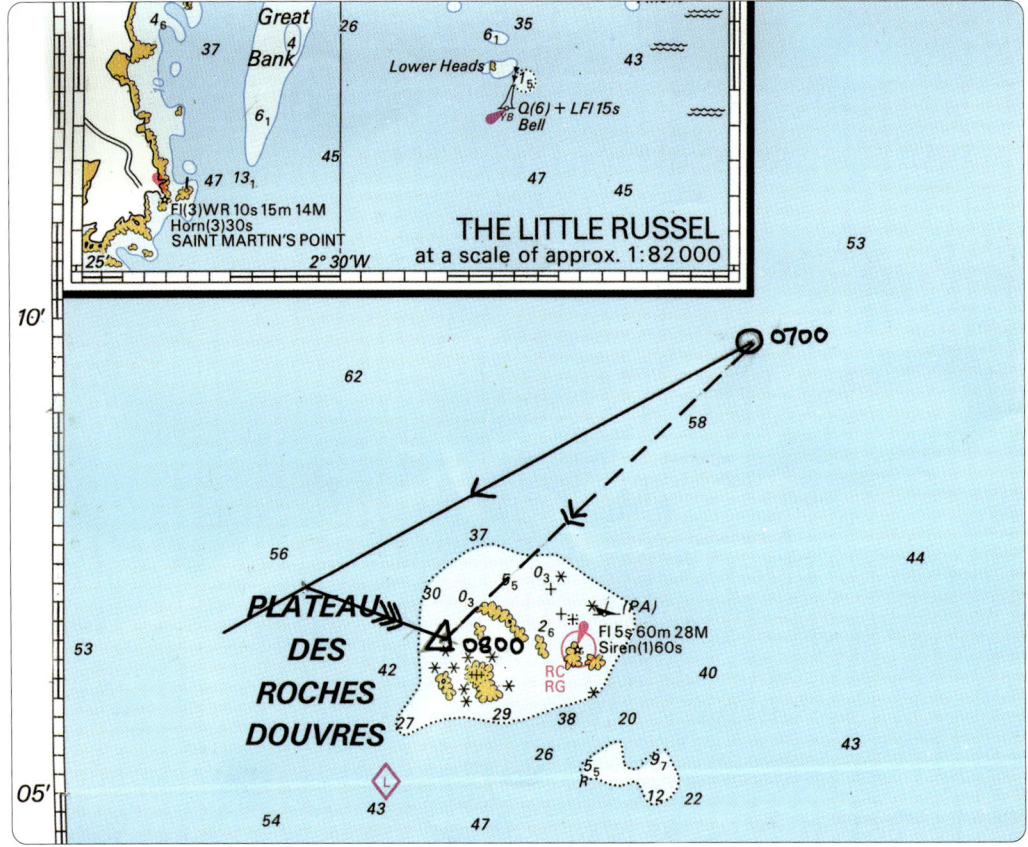

Fig A8.3 Q8.5.

8.6

See Fig A8.5 (page 60).

23 November:

HW St Helier 1608 UTC. Range 6.9m, mid range.

HW hour 1538–1638.

From ◇R◇ HW −2 1338–1438 = 097°T. Spring 2.3kn. Neap 1.0kn. Mid = 1.65kn.

◇R◇ HW −1 1438–1538 = 094°T. Spring 1.5kn. Neap 0.7kn. Mid = 1.1kn.

1st leg 060°M   =   057°T distance 4.3M.

2nd leg 095°M   =   092°T distance 7.6M.

Position of EP   =   48°41'.7N 02°16'.6W.

8.7

See Fig A8.5 (page 60).

14 October:

HW St Helier 0723 BST. Range 9.5m, springs.

a) To the east of Grand Léjon lighthouse.

b)
Heading   185°C
Deviation   +1°E
            186°M
Variation   −3°W
            183°M
Leeway   +5°
To plot   188°T (See Fig A8.4)

c) HW hour 0653–0753 BST.
◇Q◇ HW +3 0953–1053 BST = 310°T 2.1kn.

d) To port. At the closest point it will be 0.7M from the yacht.

e) The yacht is tracking directly to the post. Leeway may well have been underestimated and the strength of the stream will decrease within the bay, so it would be wise to put in a short tack once it is certain that Petit Léjon has been cleared.

YACHTMASTER EXERCISES FOR SAIL & POWER

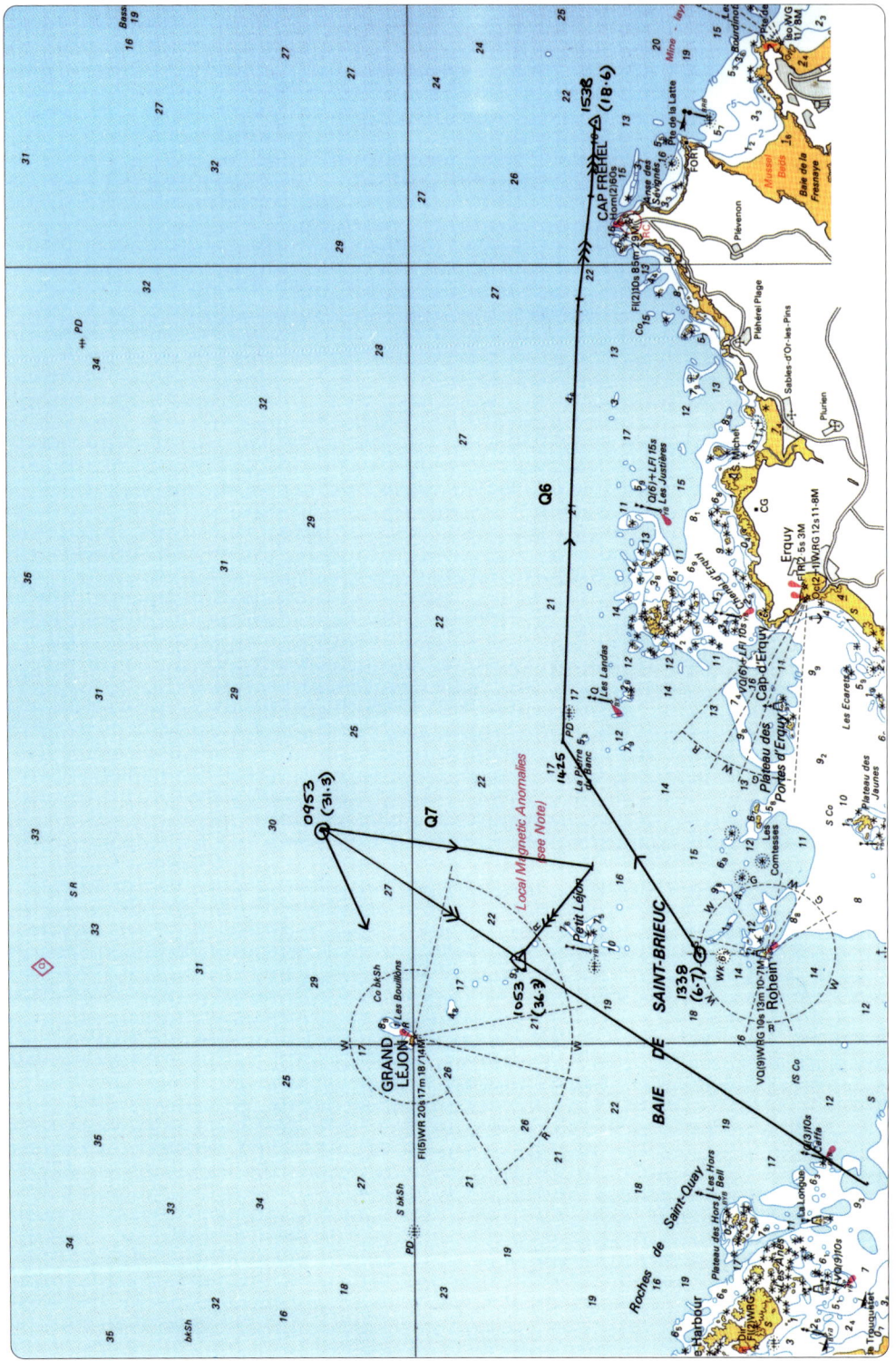

Fig A8.4 Q8.6 & 8.7.

9 ELECTRONIC NAVIGATION AND INSTRUMENTS

ANSWERS

9.1

a) Should the chartplotter fail, the navigator would have to resort to using a paper chart and traditional navigation methods if no spare GPS were carried. It would not be possible to do this if the distance sailed through the water were not recorded regularly.

b) i) The paddle wheel may be encrusted with weed and barnacles, which give a false reading.
   ii) A yacht that is well heeled in a rough sea may have the paddle wheel clear of the water some of the time. The same may happen to a motor cruiser when the hull bangs down onto waves.

c) A log that under-reads would give cause for concern as a destination (and possibly a rocky outcrop) would be reached sooner than expected.

9.2

a) When the depth sounder pulse hits a soft and squashy seabed it penetrates the softest mud at the surface rather than bouncing the pulse back to the receiver. This makes it difficult to measure the depth accurately.

b) A propeller churning through water causes turbulence and an abundance of bubbles. The sounder pulse bounces off the bubbles, not the seabed. It is common for sounders to read zero as a boat passes through the wake of power-driven craft.

9.3

a) AIS = Automatic Identification System.

b) No, because you have a receiver only and are not transmitting your position.

c) Provided the vessel is not out of range – MMSI, vessel name, position in latitude and longitude, heading, course and speed over ground and navigational status, ie stopped, under power, under sail etc.

d) There are, currently, only two available channels for the transmission of AIS information, which has led to congestion as more and more vessels become equipped with AIS. In order to reduce traffic it is wise to switch off the AIS when in harbour.

9.4

The GPS antenna gives a better performance if it is mounted low down on the craft. If mounted at the top of the mast, rolling in a rough sea will cause signal bounce.

9.5

a) i) The display is stabilised using an electronic compass so that the picture will remain steady and not swing from side to side as the boat yaws. This makes it easier to calculate whether a risk of collision exists.

b) ii) the smaller aluminium boat will reflect the radar beams well, provided that the hull is not curved. Radar beams pass straight through GRP so the motor cruiser would require an effective radar reflector.

c) You are likely to have more difficulty because the beam width of your set is about 5° wide and his beam is narrower at just over 1°. This makes it more difficult to distinguish harbour entrances at a distance. You will have to get closer to the entrance than your friend for it to 'open up'.

d) The theoretical horizon is calculated by taking the square root of the height of the antenna and multiplying it by 2.25 = 6.75 nautical miles. The lower part of objects further away than this will be below the horizon.

e) 'North-up' mode means that the radar display is aligned so that the picture looks like the chart, with north, not heading, at the top of the display.

f) 'Sea Clutter: This control reduces the gain near the ship so that in choppy seas it will reduce the resultant clutter up to about two miles. It should be used with extreme caution as it will eliminate a 'legitimate' contact, so should always be reduced to zero as soon as possible.

9.6

a) MARPA is the abbreviation for Mini Automatic Radar Plotting Aid. This clever device tracks the progress of a highlighted contact on the display and calculates its true course and speed and how close it will pass.

b) CPA = Closest Point of Approach.

This gives a good indication whether a risky situation is developing. Don't forget that this value is calculated using current data. Any change of course and speed by either vessel will change the CPA. Continual monitoring is therefore necessary.

c) TCPA = Time to Closest Point of Approach.

9.7

Yes. As the set transmits a signal it has to be included on your ship's radio licence.

9.8

There are three companies who make electronic charts for the main plotter manufacturers. Navionics, Garmin (Blue chart) and Jepperson (C-Map) all offer updating facilities but how you do it depends on the make and the package of charts you have. The majority of charts on plotters are now updated automatically via the internet with an annual subscription. For older sets you probably have to buy an updated SD or compact flash card. It is vital you have the latest charts. Don't be put off by the cost – repairs to your boat after you have made the mistake of using old charts will cost a lot more!

Fig A9.1 Blue chart displayed on a Garmin plotter.

10 PILOTAGE

ANSWERS

10.1

a) A transit line using the right-hand edge of Burhou Island and Great Nannel clears both Ozard Rock and the Corbet group. Alternatively, a clearing bearing on the right-hand edge of Burhou of no less than 008°M gives a similar clearance if Great Nannel cannot be identified.

b) Use the transit already marked on the chart, but have the hand-bearing compass handy to check the bearing of 083°M on the end of the breakwater in case the Château is not easily visible.

10.2

See Fig A10.1.

a) The boat is somewhere in the middle of the Paternoster Rocks where there are many rocks that cover and uncover.

b) One possible explanation is that the compass could have been damaged or a mobile phone may have been wedged near it, but this deviation would have become apparent on the GPS display as the cross track error increased.
The most likely cause is an error in entering the waypoint. If 49°17′.6N were entered instead of 49°16′.7N, the boat would be led straight across the rocks.

c) The skipper should have drawn the route on the chart so that the bearing and distance between each waypoint could be checked. It would also have been wise to take a back bearing on Sorel Point lighthouse as the Desormes Buoy would probably not be visible at almost 4M distant.

10.3

Illustration a). See Fig A10.2.

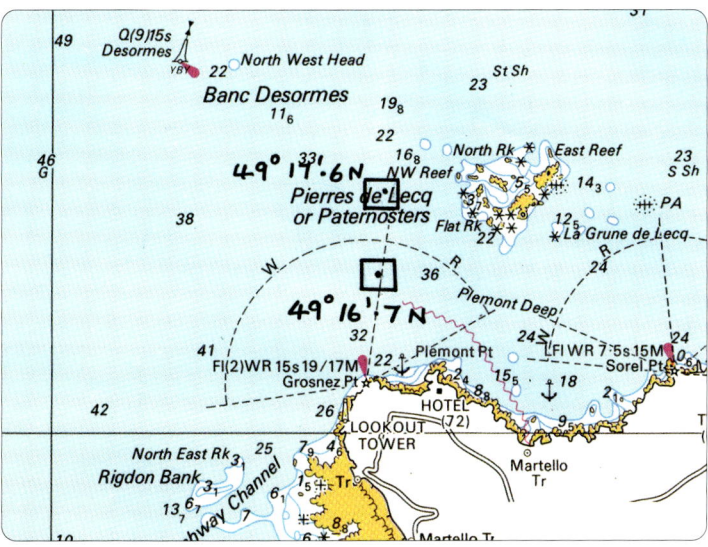

Fig A10.1 Q10.2.

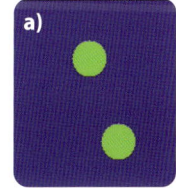

Fig A10.2 Leading lights.

10.4

a) Yes. The eastern end of the island is closed to the public from 1 April to 30 June. It is now July, so a visit is possible.

b) Yes. The islands are not considered to be a port of entry and the boat is entering French territory from outside the EU (Jersey). The boat must visit an entry port, ie Granville or St Malo, before going on to Îles Chausey.

c) There is no harbourmaster and no VHF channel in use.

d) Yes, there is a bar.

e) 7.2m. The channel dries 4.4m + 1.3m draught + 1.5m clearance.

10.5

All movements are prohibited except for the large ship that is departing.

10.6

Sunday 20 June:

a) HW St Malo 0831 FStanT.
HW Granville +5mins = 0936 FSumT.
Access to marina = HW −2½ to HW +3½ = 0706 to 1306.

b) A sharp turning out of the marina hides other vessels from view.

c) No, entry and exit must be under power.

d) On a digital display on top of the southern breakwater.

e) Shallowest part of Granville entrance channel dries 2.0m.

Access from marina is at 0706.
HW St Malo FStanT	0831	10.8m	LW 2.7m	Mid range
Differences for Granville	+0005	+0.6m	+0.2m	
	0836	11.4m	2.9m	
Plus 1 hour for FSumT.	0936			

Height of tide at 0706 = 7.6m.
Depth of water over the drying 2.0m patch = 5.6m.

f) Yes, it is possible.

HW St Malo (FSumT) 0931 10.8m LW 2.7m
Time of arrival = 1400 = HW +4½ hours.
Height of tide = 5.2m.
Sill dries 2.0m therefore depth over the sill at 1400 = 3.2m.
Depth required = Draught 1.8m plus clearance of 1.0m = 2.8m.

g) Channel 9.

h) Yes, there are waiting buoys outside Les Bas-Sablons Marina.

11 COLLISION REGULATIONS

ANSWERS

11.1

The rules apply to:

'All vessels upon the high seas and in all waters connected therewith navigable by seagoing vessels.'

(Note: The rules would not normally apply on lakes such as Windermere but most local authorities adopt the rules within their bye-laws.)

11.2

The regulations do not mention the words 'right of way'. They talk about the 'stand on' and the 'give-way' vessels but also make it quite clear that everyone is responsible for avoiding a collision – not just the 'give-way vessel'.

11.3

a) Both these power-driven vessels should alter course. Both should alter course to starboard and both sound one short blast on the horn to tell everyone what is intended.

(Note: Only power-driven craft give a sound signal when altering course.)

b) Yacht B is the give-way vessel as she is overtaking A. The yacht should pass astern of boat A. Remember that ANY vessel overtaking another becomes the give-way vessel.

c) Motorboat B gives way to motorboat A. She should give one short blast on the horn and alter course to starboard to pass behind A or slow down to let A pass ahead.

(Note: Boat B can see the red port light of boat A. The rhyme 'If to starboard red appear, it is your duty to keep clear' is a good one to remember.)

d) Boat A is the give-way vessel as, although on the same tack as B, it is to windward. The skipper should ease sheets and bear away to pass behind B.

e) Yacht A is the give-way vessel as it is on port tack. The skipper should either tack onto a parallel course or ease sheets to bear away around the stern of B.

f) Power-driven vessel A is the give-way vessel. She should sound the appropriate sound signal and alter course to avoid Yacht B, or slow down to let B pass ahead.

11.4

Rule 6 – Safe speed states that the skipper should consider the following:

a) the state of visibility.
b) the traffic density including concentrations of fishing vessels and other vessels.
c) the manoeuvrability of the vessel (stopping distance and turning circle).
d) the state of wind, sea and current and proximity of navigational hazards.
e) the draught in relation to the available depth of water.
f) at night, the presence of background lights such as from shore lights.

YACHTMASTER EXERCISES FOR SAIL & POWER

11.5

Rule 9b – Narrow channels say that *vessels under 20 metres in length* and *sailing vessels* must avoid impeding the safe passage of a vessel that can safely navigate only within a narrow channel or fairway.

11.6

This signal is the International Code flag Alpha, which means:

'I have a diver down. Keep well clear at slow speed.'

11.7

The heading must be at right angles. This means that the crossing vessel presents a beam-on aspect to shipping within the lane and reaches the far side of the lane more quickly than the vessel on a right-angled ground track, as shown in Fig A11.1.

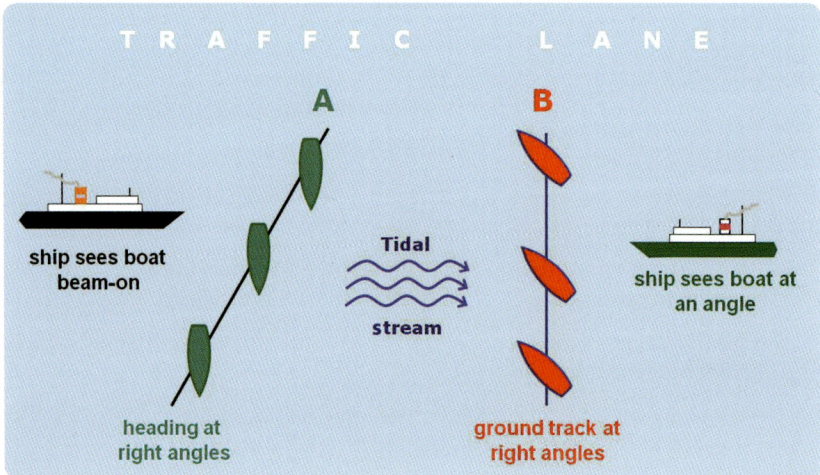

Fig A11.1 Crossing shipping lanes.

11.8

a) At anchor (any length).

b) Restricted in its ability to manoeuvre.

c) Motorsailing.

d) Aground.

e) Constrained by draught.

f) Gear extending to more than 150m horizontally from a fishing vessel.

g) Fishing or trawling.

h) Not under command.

i) Length of tow exceeds 200m.

ANSWERS • COLLISION REGULATIONS

11.9

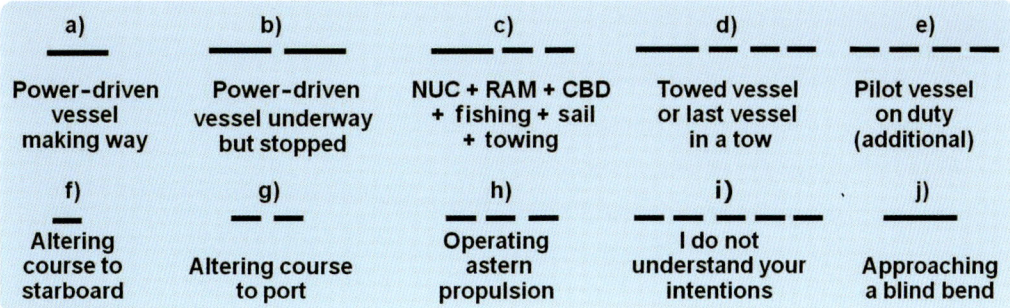

Fig A11.2 Meanings for sound signals.

11.10

A   Power-driven vessel, seen from ahead, probably more than 50m in length, underway.

B   At anchor, port aspect, probably more than 50m in length.

(Note: When at anchor, the light at the bow is higher than the aft light.)

C   Constrained by draught, port aspect, probably more than 50m in length, underway or making way.

D   Power-driven vessel engaged in towing, seen from ahead. It is *EITHER* under 50m in length with a tow of more than 200m, *OR* more than 50m in length with a tow of less than 200m, underway or making way.

E   Restricted in its ability to manoeuvre, starboard aspect, under 50m in length, making way.

(Note: Vessels restricted in their ability to manoeuvre, not under command, fishing and trawling turn their sidelights OFF when not making way through the water.)

F   Fishing, stopped (making no way), aspect unknown, no gear more than 150m.

G   Not under command, length and aspect unknown, underway but stopped, ie drifting.

H   Sailing vessel, port aspect, underway or making way.

I   Trawling, starboard aspect, under 50m in length, making way.

J   A stern light of a vessel of any length *OR* an all-round anchor light of a vessel under 50m in length *OR* boat under oars *OR* a small power-driven vessel under 7m and under 7kn.

K   Fishing, head-on, making way.

L   Pilot vessel on duty, *EITHER* at anchor *OR* underway or making way, seen from astern.

11.11

a)   Sidelights, stern light and a steaming light.

b)   Sidelights, stern light and a steaming light. (Under 12m the last two may be combined.)

c)   An all-round white light.

d)   Sidelights and a stern light *OR* a tricolour lantern carried at the top of the mast.

67

11.12

a) SOS in Morse code by torch or sound.

b) A distress alert from a VHF DSC radio.

c) The spoken word 'Mayday' on VHF radio.

d) Emergency Position Indicating Radio Beacon (EPIRB).

e) A red parachute rocket or hand-held red flare.

f) Orange smoke.

g) Slowly and repeatedly raising and lowering the arms.

h) Deployment of an AIS SART.

i) The international code flags NC.

j) Continuous sounding of a foghorn.

12 METEOROLOGY

ANSWERS

12.1

a) 1.25m to 2.5m.

b) Gale force 8.

c) Force 6.

d) 2 to 5M.

e) Between 6 and 12 hours after the time of issue.

f) The centre of low pressure will pass through the sea area with the wind altering direction as expected in a depression.

12.2

b) and c).

12.3

To the south of you. Buys Ballot's law says: 'If you stand with your back to the wind in the northern hemisphere, the area of low pressure is on your left-hand side.'

12.4

a) Force 3.

b) Force 5.

12.5

a) Cloud C. This is high cirrostratus cloud with the sun shining through it causing a halo.

b) Cloud B. This is cumulonimbus cloud, which has fanned out to form an anvil. Under this cloud the wind will be very gusty and squally. These clouds will decrease in size and frequency as the weather settles down and showers die out.

12.6

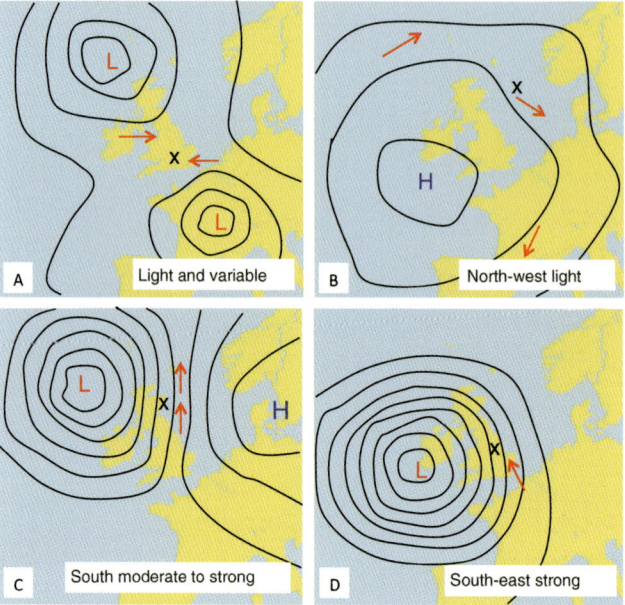

Fig A12.1 Wind speed and direction.

12.7

Sea fog

a) When there is warm, damp air blowing over a cold surface such as the sea.

b) In the late spring and early summer when the sea is still cold and the warm tropical air comes up from the south.

c) A wind strength of over Force 5 should lift the fog off the sea surface to give low stratus cloud, or a change to a polar air-stream will clear it.

d) Wind and tidal stream invariably strengthen around headlands where the seabed is uneven. The water is roughened, which causes turbulence in the air above it. This turbulence helps to cool the air below the dew point and fog forms. In less turbulent areas the fog may not form.

Radiation fog

e) This type of fog typically forms in autumn and winter when the land cools quickly.

f) Yes, when the air is heated it can hold more water vapour invisibly and the fog disperses on all but the worst days.

ANSWERS • METEOROLOGY

12.8

a) South to south-east.

b) A deep depression.

c) This is an occluded front formed when the leading edge of cold air catches up with the warm air and pushes it upwards. See page 102 of *Yachtmaster for Sail and Power*.

d) The pressure will be falling in sea area Fair Isle.

e) Sea area Tyne is in the warm sector so the visibility will be poor with intermittent rain and drizzle.

f) The cold front has passed through sea area Fastnet so the visibility will be good.

g) Cromarty is close to the warm front so the cloud is likely to be nimbostratus.

h) A cold front showing the boundary between warm and cold air.

i) This is the early formation of another depression, known as a wave depression. The warm air coming up from the south around the high pressure is rising above the cold air. As the air rises it will be affected by the Coriolis force and will begin to circulate in an anticlockwise direction. The weather over the UK does not look as if it will be settled for a day or two.

12.9

a) Your diagram should look similar to that in Fig A12.2.

b) The wind will tend to veer during the day.

c) The breeze will be strongest in the mid-afternoon when the land is well heated and the greatest circulation has been set up.

d) As the sun sets the land will cool and the breeze will die. A land breeze may blow lightly seaward but if not the conditions will be calm.

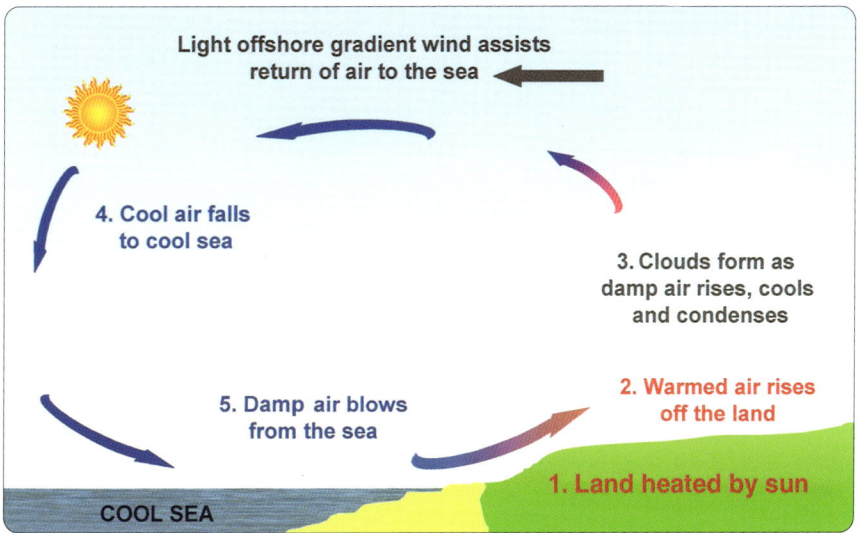

Fig A12.2

12.10

a) The origin, weather model it is based on, alongside the time and date of the forecast.

b) If they are all very similar the prediction is in all likelihood correct. If they are widely different, then there is very little certainty.

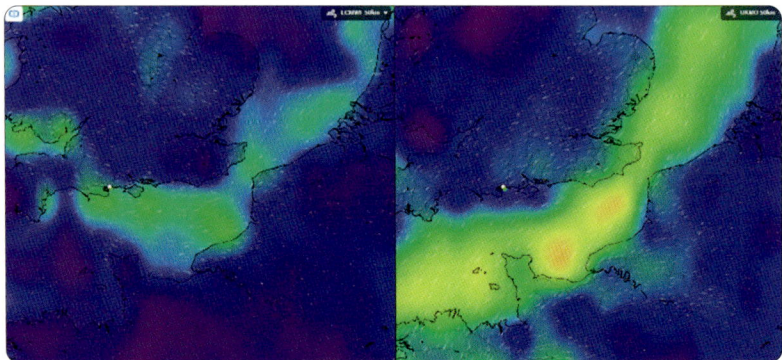

Fig A12.3 Two differing forecast models.

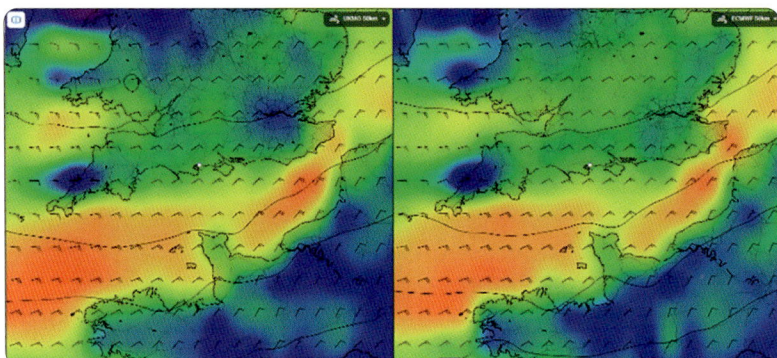

Fig A12.4 Two similar forecasts.

13 SAFETY AND COMMUNICATIONS

ANSWERS

13.1

a)
- Open the cover, which is either red or labelled 'Distress'.
- Press the red button once and, if there is time, select the type of distress situation from a list of categories.
- Press the red button again for 5 seconds or until the 'Distress alert sent' message appears on the display.

b) The MMSI (identification number), the time (in UTC) and the boat's position in latitude and longitude. In addition, if selected by the casualty, the nature of distress.

c) Digitally first, and then by voice after the voice Mayday.

d) 15 seconds to allow time for the receiving station to grab a pen to write down the voice message.

e)
> Mayday, Mayday, Mayday.
>
> This is Motor Cruiser *Sinking Feeling*, *Sinking Feeling*, *Sinking Feeling*.
>
> MMSI 235899983. Callsign Two Zulu Xray Yankee.
>
> Mayday *Sinking Feeling*. MMSI 235899983 Callsign Two Zulu Xray Yankee.
>
> My position is 50°10′.4N 001°18′.6W.
>
> Holed and sinking.
>
> Require immediate assistance.
>
> 4 persons on board. Abandoning to liferaft.
>
> Over.

13.2

a) Normally the helicopter will make an approach on the port side of the casualty as the pilot and the door are on the right-hand side of the aircraft. However, a powerless, wallowing craft may not head into wind, in which case the helicopter will try to approach into wind as the short mast of a motor cruiser does not restrict the approach angle.

b) The crew will be told:
  i) that either a weighted line or the diver on a wire will be lowered to the deck.
  ii) not to attach the line to the vessel.
  iii) to take control of the line and to assist the diver onto the deck.

(Note: In the case of the crew of *Sinking Feeling*, they are most likely to be sent up into the helicopter in pairs in a rescue strop with the diver remaining on the craft until everyone is safe.)

c) A handheld red pinpoint flare or an orange smoke.

d) A parachute flare. Helicopters do not appreciate an attempt to shoot them down!

13.3

a) Channel 16.

b) Channel 13.

c) Channel 67.

d) Channel 80.

13.4

a) Gale and strong wind warnings.
Shipping forecast extracts of local areas, inshore waters forecasts and two day forecasts.
Information on firing times at ranges (Gunfax) and activity in submarine exercise areas (Subfax).

b) ii) Three hourly with a new inshore waters forecast every six hours.

Fig A13.1 Rescuer on the way.

13.5

a) This refers to the 'Angle of Vanishing Stability' – the angle above which the boat no longer regains an upright position and finds it easier to turn upside down. Those craft with a high AVS can heel to a greater angle before they lose stability, and are therefore more suitable for comfortable, safe ocean cruising where it is difficult to find shelter in heavy weather. They may not be as fast as a boat with a lower AVS.

b) This is an Emergency Position Indicating Radio Beacon (EPIRB), which, when activated, uses the frequency of 406MHz to send a signal to a receiving station via a satellite. The ground station contacts Falmouth Coastguard who maintains the national registry of EPIRB serial numbers, so that the casualty may be identified easily. Falmouth Coastguard then alerts local rescue services to help the casualty.

c) The main advantages of the latest generation of 406MHZ EPIRBs with AIS

   1. Reducing the search radius of your distress to 10 metres.

   2. Alerts other vessels fitted with AIS within range.

   3. Return Link Service (RLS).

   4. Strobe and infrared strobe.

It can even be connected to your phone which tells you when and where you last did a self-test along with the battery state.

If you acquire a secondhand EPIRB you should inform HM Coastguard at Falmouth about the change of ownership – this is a legal requirement.

Fig A13.2 An EPIRB.

ANSWERS • SAFETY AND COMMUNICATIONS

13.6

a) A red parachute flare (top of Fig 13.3 on page 29) that can ascend to about 300m.

b) An orange smoke signal (bottom left of Fig 13.3 on page 29).

c) A handheld pinpoint red flare (right of Fig 13.3 on page 29).

13.7

Between three or four years, depending on the time of year that the pack is purchased.

13.8

a) The torch bearer is flashing the morse code letter U (Uniform) which is internationally recognised as a warning that you are running into danger.

b) You should stop and/or retrace your route while you sort things out.

13.9

The aircraft is telling the skipper that his assistance is no longer required.

These signals may be found on pages 171 and 172 of *Yachtmaster for Sail and Power*.

14 PLANNING AND MAKING PASSAGES

Passage planning does not always have a definitive answer – the answers given here are one option considered to give a successful passage. If your answers differ a little, they are probably not wrong, just a different interpretation.

14

The plan must involve the four key stages.

1. Appraisal – Is it feasible? The gathering of information.

2. Planning – The making of a detailed plan.

3. Execution – Undertaking the plan adjusting for any corrections.

4. Monitoring – Is the plan working?

PASSAGE 1

14.1

Sunday 5 September:

a) St Helier HW 1054 BST. Range 6.3m, mid range.

b) St Helier HW −3hrs to HW +3hrs = 0754 to 1354.

c) Yes. La Collette Yacht Basin has 24hr access with a 1.8m minimum depth.

d) Distance is approximately 37M. Passage time approx 1hr 30mins in calm sea.

e) HW Dover 1558 BST.

f) The stream is favourable for the whole length of the passage from 1130 to 1330. Before 1130 there is an adverse stream along the south coast of Jersey, and after 1330 there is a counter current off Diélette.

g) Yes, it is restricted by the depths in the outer harbour but mostly at springs. The narrative for Diélette says that it is dredged to CD +0.5m, but the chart shows it dredged to chart datum. We must therefore assume that it dries 0.5m, which is the worst case. As 5 September is mid range, we can look at the differences data:

St Malo MLWN = 4.2m less 0.7m at Diélette = 3.5m.
St Malo MLWS = 1.5m less 0.3m at Diélette = 1.2m.
Take a mid range figure between these two = 2.35m.

The cruiser is therefore likely to float at all states of the tide on 5 September, provided that the recommended route is used once inside the breakwater.

h) HW Dover 1558 BST. Diélette HW is HW Dover −4hrs 30mins = 1128 BST.
Access is HW +/−3hrs = 0828 to 1428 BST

i) Dangers:
   - Ships and ferries leaving St Helier. Watch the traffic lights.
   - Rocks at St Helier's entrance.
   - Rough water off Point Corbière.

ANSWERS • PLANNING AND MAKING PASSAGES

- Rough water off Rigdon Bank on the north-west corner of Jersey.
- The Paternoster Rocks off the north coast of Jersey.
- Local magnetic anomalies affecting the compass.
- Rocky bank to the north-east of Diélette's entrance.
- Traffic leaving round the corner of the breakwater at Diélette.

j) Close to 1130, which will give ample time to benefit from the fair stream.

k) Tune to VHF Channel 18 to obtain information about wind speed and direction at St Helier Pierheads.

14.2

Waypoint 1 to 2	277°T	4.8M.
Waypoint 2 to 3	353°T	4.0M.
Waypoint 3 to 4	030°T	4.9M.
Waypoint 4 to 5	041°T	19.4M.
Waypoint 5 to 6	070°T	1.5M.

14.3

See Fig A14.1.

a) 49°29′.0N 002°02′.5W.

b) HW Dover 1558 BST. Mid range.
HW hour = 1528–1628. HW −3 = 1228–1328.

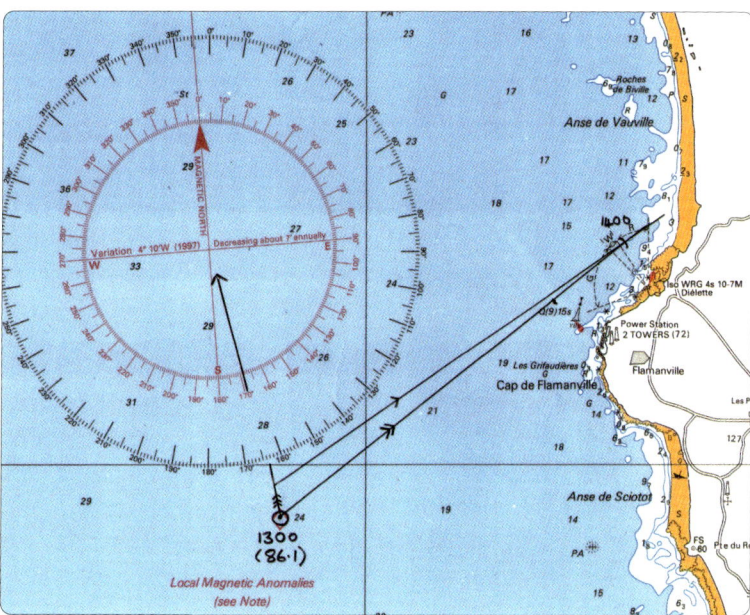

Fig A14.1 Plot for Q14.3.

YACHTMASTER EXERCISES FOR SAIL & POWER

The stream charts show that two arrows and rates cover the passage area.
The average direction and rate for mid range = 348°T 1.5kn (20 mins 0.5M).
Course to steer = 057°T + 3°W variation = 060°M – 1°E deviation = 059°C.

(Note: A 20-minute tidal vector has been plotted, ie both boat speed and rate of stream have been divided by three – same triangle but smaller scale.)

c) Formula for ETA at the buoy:

Distance to go ÷ distance covered in 20mins × 20 = elapsed time
6.6M ÷ 8.3M × 20 = 16mins run. ETA = 1316 BST.

14.4

Yes it does, there is a 30-ton crane, although you may not be very lucky on a Sunday afternoon!

PASSAGE 2

14.5

Wednesday 4 August:

HW St Peter Port 0905 BST 9.2m:

a) Use the table in extract 14 at the back of this book to give heights over the marina sill.
Water required = 1.9m draught + 0.5m clearance = 2.4m.
Depth over the sill at HW –2½hrs = 2.08m and at HW –2hrs = 3.05m.
There is sufficient depth at HW +/–2hrs 15mins = 0650 to 1120 BST.

b) Visitors may wait on the waiting pontoon or, if additional depth is required, on pontoons 1 to 5 (see the harbour chart in Extract 13 at the back of the book).

14.6

a) Distance to the south-west corner of Jersey is approximately 19½ miles and 34 miles more to Granville.

b) It will take just over 3hrs to complete the first part provided that the wind is not force 5 on the nose – when it would take longer. A further 5¾hrs will be needed for the second part (excluding the tidal stream).

14.7

a) St Malo is the standard port for Granville and HW St Malo is at 2158 BST.

b) HW Granville is at HW St Malo +5 minutes = 2203 BST.

c) Access to Granville Marina is HW Granville –2½hrs to HW +3½hrs = 1933 to 0133 (5 August).

d) HW Dover = 1435 BST. Springs.

e) The best time to arrive, thinking of the stream alone, would be by HW Dover +4½hrs (1905) as all the tidal arrows point to Granville, but the marina would not be open at that time. Arriving at HW Dover +5½hrs would just about be acceptable as there is under 1kn of stream against us on the run into the port. After that, the stream picks up against us.

ANSWERS • PLANNING AND MAKING PASSAGES

14.8

a) The latest time to leave the marina is 1120, so exit before then is essential.

b) If the wind is still in the south the passage to the Corbière corner will be a beat, so it would be wise to leave a little before then even though the stream outside the harbour is setting north.

If the wind has already veered, then we can wait in the outer harbour until the stream turns south at about 1230. We should then cover the 20M to south-west Jersey by 1600 to take slack or weak favourable stream along the south Jersey coast – nicely on schedule.

First thoughts are that there will be little stream advantage during the first 20M because it is a cross-stream, but once south of Jersey the strong favourable stream should be carried to Granville – and any time lost earlier can be made up.

14.9

A cold front is passing over the area. This is a typical forecast – a veer in the wind, increased visibility and rain turning to showers after the front has passed.

ON PASSAGE

14.10

See Fig A14.2.

Wednesday 4 August:

HW St Helier 0958 BST. Springs.
HW hour 0928–1028.

◇J HW +3 1228–1328 = 004°T 0.7kn 1/2hr 0.35M

◇J HW +4 1328–1428 = 282°T 0.7kn 1/2hr 0.35M

Course:	135°C
Deviation	+5°E
Magnetic	140°M
Leeway	−10°
Variation	−3°W
Plotted	127°T

a) EP 49°22′.6N 02°21′.4W.

b) The difference in the two positions could be for a number of reasons. The tide may have turned early, the leeway may have been overestimated, or perhaps the helmsman finds sailing to windward difficult.

14.11

See Fig A14.3 (page 81).

HW Dover 1435 BST HW hour 1405–1505
HW Dover +5 = 1905–2005. 100°T. 1.9kn. Boat speed 7kn.

a) Course to steer = 142°T + 3°W = 145°M − 4°E = 141°C.

b) SOG = 8.6kn.

YACHTMASTER EXERCISES FOR SAIL & POWER

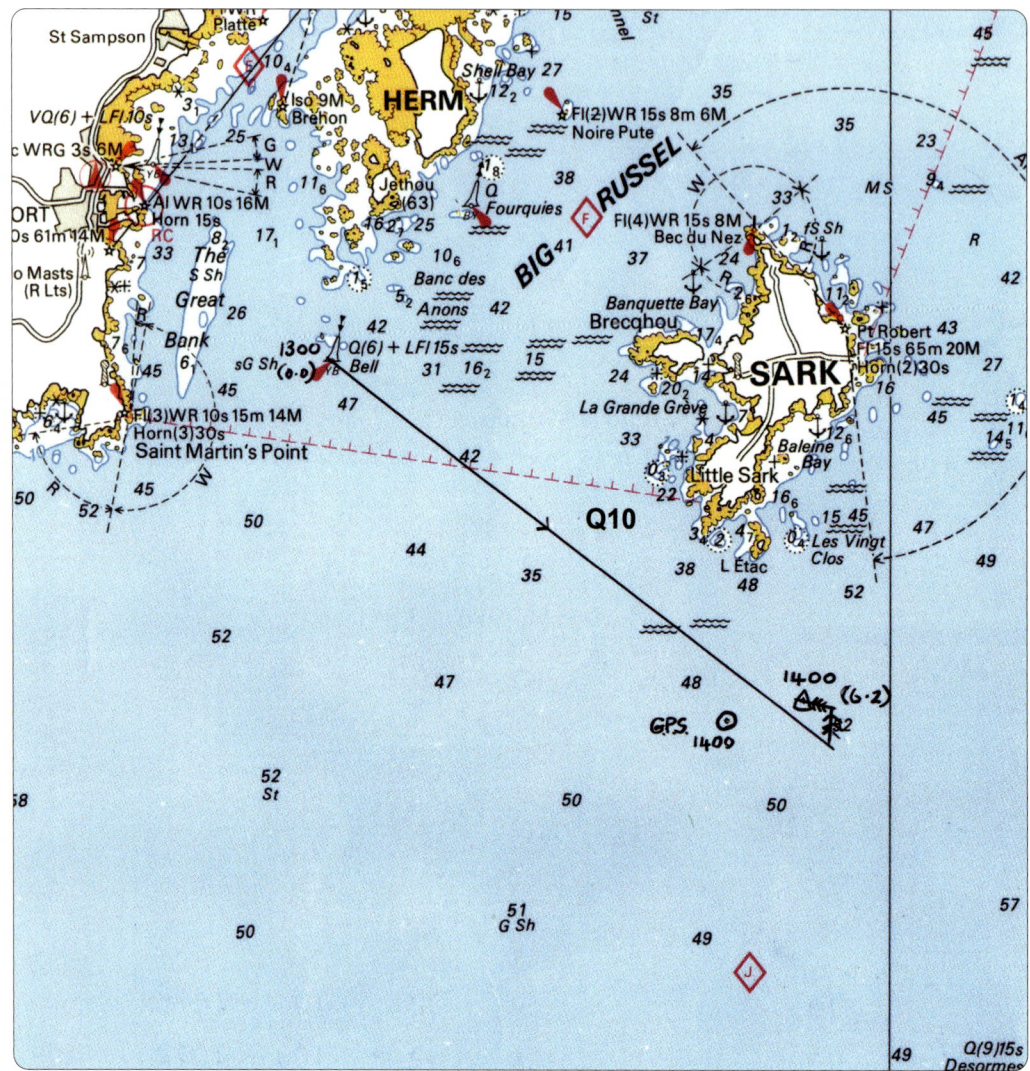

Fig A14.2 Plot for Q14.10.

14.12

a) The dangers are: rocks and lobster pots off Pointe du Roc, and traffic coming round the blind bend outside the marina.

b) The skipper can check depth calculations by sighting the illuminated tidal height display board on the southern harbour wall.

ANSWERS • PLANNING AND MAKING PASSAGES

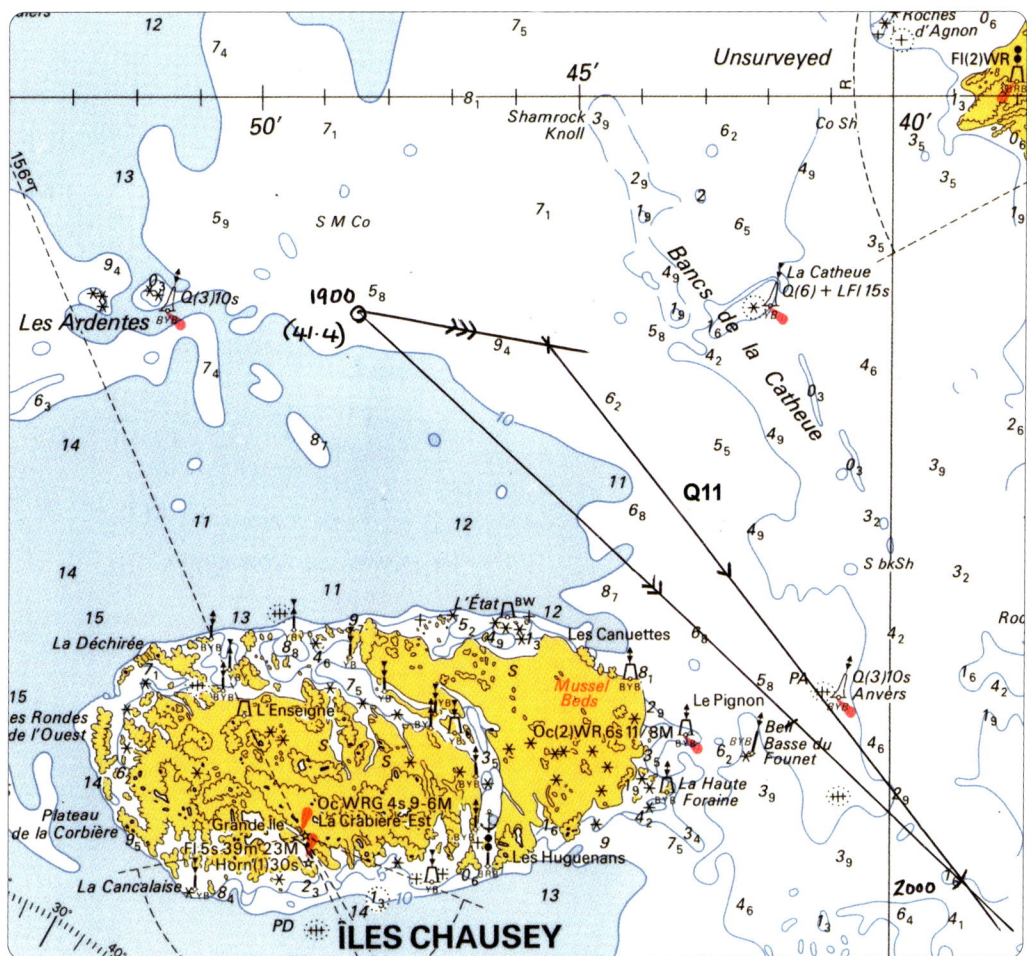

Fig A14.3 Plot for Q14.11.

15 CHARTWORK TEST PAPER 1

15.1

See Fig A15.1.

Position at 1010 UTC is 49°41'.0N 002°09'.7W.

15.2

See Fig A15.1.

Tuesday 2 November:

HW St Helier 0842 UTC. Range 6.5m, close to mid range.
HW hour 0812–0912 UTC.

Ⓑ HW +2 1012–1112 031°T 4.2kn (spring) 2.0kn (neap) 3.1kn (mid).

a) Course to steer 080°T + 3°W = 083°M.

b) Slack at 1212 UTC, and clearly unfavourable by 1312 UTC (HW +5).

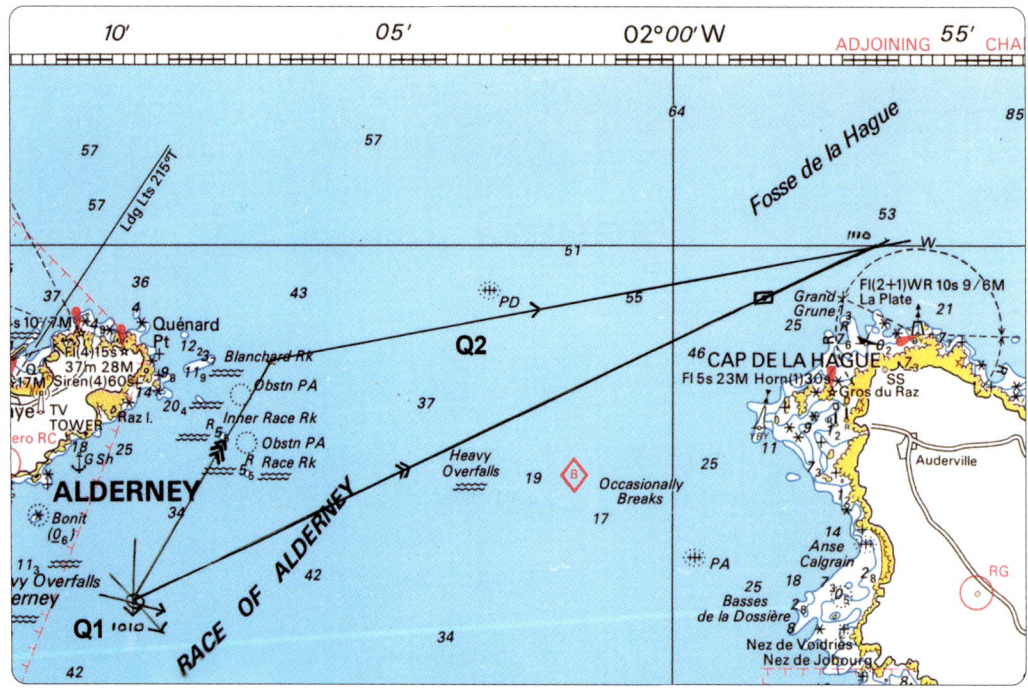

Fig A15.1 Q15.1 & 15.2.

15.3

See Fig A15.3.

Thursday 21 October:

HW St Helier 1226 BST. Range 4.2m, neaps.
HW hour 1156–1256.

◇ HW –5 0656–0756 203°T 1.4kn.

◇ HW –4 0756–0856 172°T 1.0kn.

1st Course: 270°C – 4°W deviation – 3°W variation + 10° leeway = 273°T.
2nd Course: 170°C + 2°E deviation – 3°W variation – 10° leeway = 159°T.

EP at 0800 = 49°35′.1N 02°29′.7W.
EP at 0900 = 49°30′.2N 02°27′.0W.

15.4

Saturday 25 September:

a) Cherbourg FStanT Range 3.2m.

	HW 0625	5.4m	LW 1300	2.2m
Cherbourg	HW 0625	5.4m	LW 1300	2.2m
Difference	+0103	+0.2m	+0052	0.0m
Barfleur FSumT	0828	5.6m	1452	2.2m

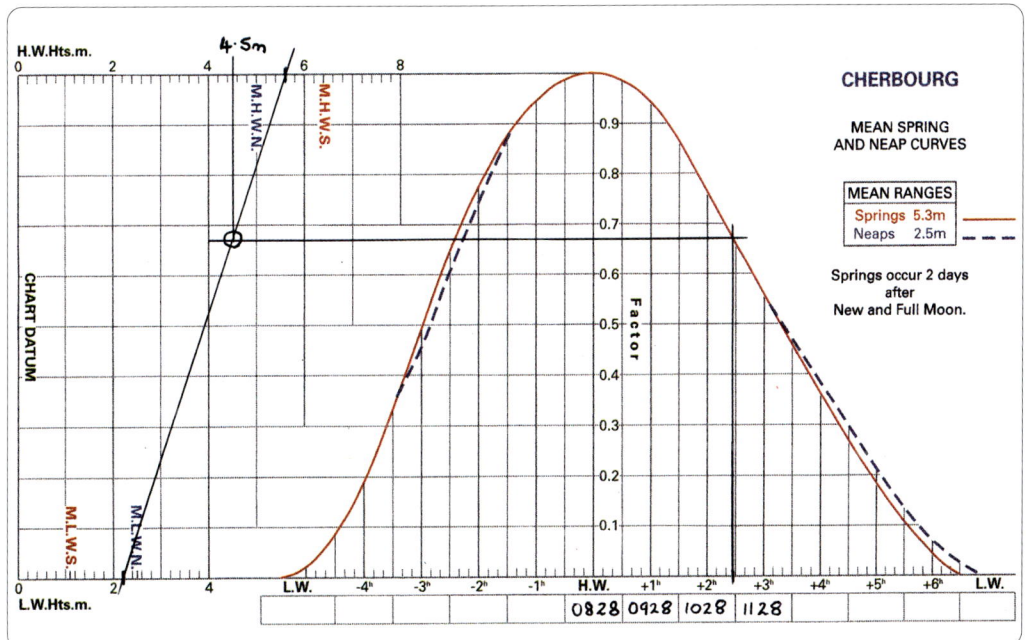

Fig A15.2 Q15.4b.

YACHTMASTER EXERCISES FOR SAIL & POWER

b) See Fig A15.2. From Cherbourg curve with data for Barfleur:
Height of tide at 1055 FSumT = 4.5m.

c) Fall to LW (2.2m) = 2.3m.
Depth of water in which to anchor:
Fall 2.3m + Draught 1.8m + Clearance 1.0m = 5.1m.

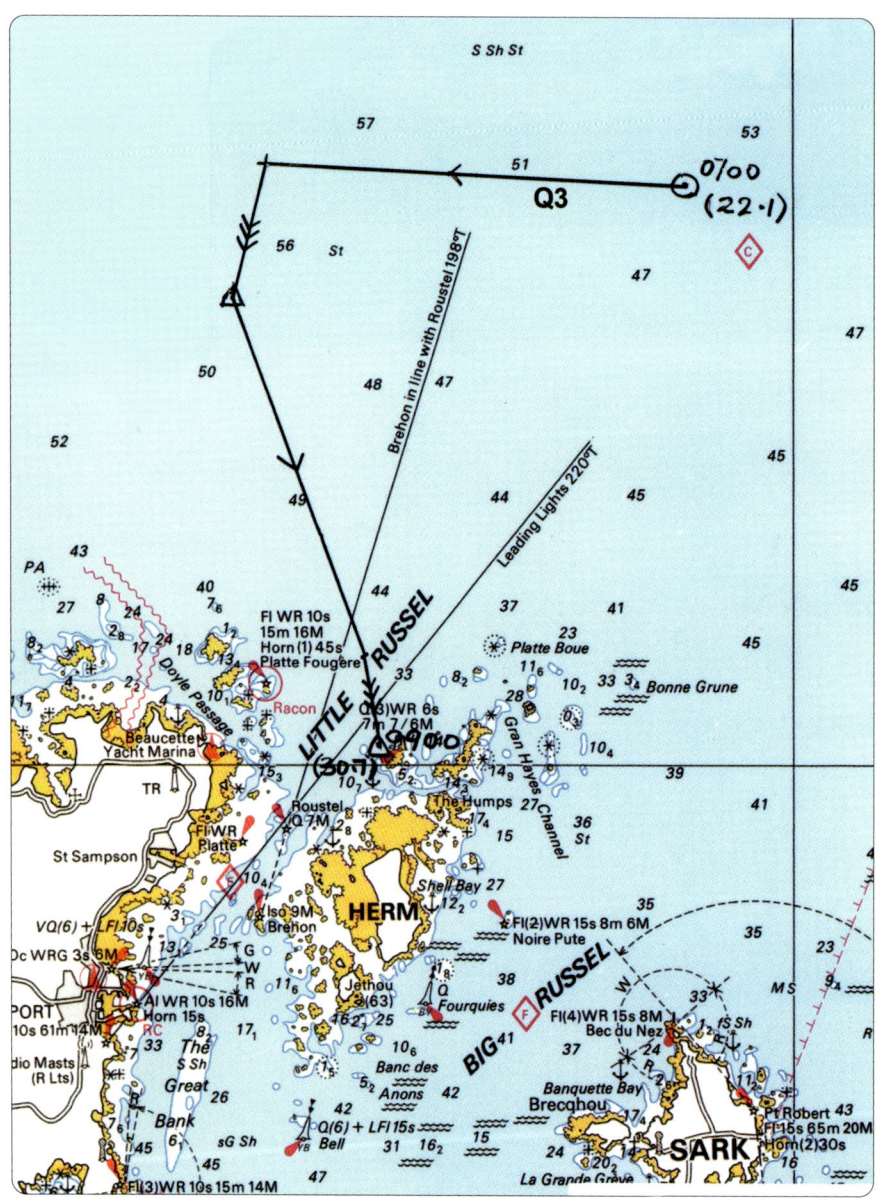

Fig A15.3 Q15.3.

16 CHARTWORK TEST PAPER 2

ANSWERS

16.1

See Fig A16.1.

The position at 1450 = 49°16'.3N 002°06'.6W.

16.2

See Fig A16.1.

Sunday 12 September:

Course to plot = 023° − 1°W deviation − 3°W variation = 019°T.

a) HW St Helier 1818 BST. Range 6.7, mid range.
   HW hour 1748–1848.
   ◇ HW −3 1448–1548 = 117°T 3.0kn (spring) 1.2kn (neap).
   It is mid range, which = 2.1kn; ½hr = 1.05M.
   EP at 1520 = 49°21'.4N 02°02'.1W.

b) 1.0M.

c) Distance 3.2M ÷ SOG 12.0kn x 60 = 16mins + 1450 = 1506 BST.

d) The skipper could:
   - draw a clearing bearing of 215°M on the TV mast, which would give 1M clearance;
   - insert a waypoint north of the rocks and steer to keep the waypoint on a safe and steady bearing, or draw a clearing bearing from the waypoint.

16.3

See Fig A16.2.

Thursday 14 October:

HW Dover 1151 BST. Range 5.9m, springs.

Distance to go = 9M, therefore approx 2hrs at 4kn.
HW hour 1121–1221.
HW +3 1421–1521 149°T 2.0kn.
HW +4 1521–1621 149°T 2.0kn.
Course to steer (no leeway) = 190°T + 3°W = 193°M.

Aim into the SE wind to correct for leeway, so subtract 5° = 188°M.

YACHTMASTER EXERCISES FOR SAIL & POWER

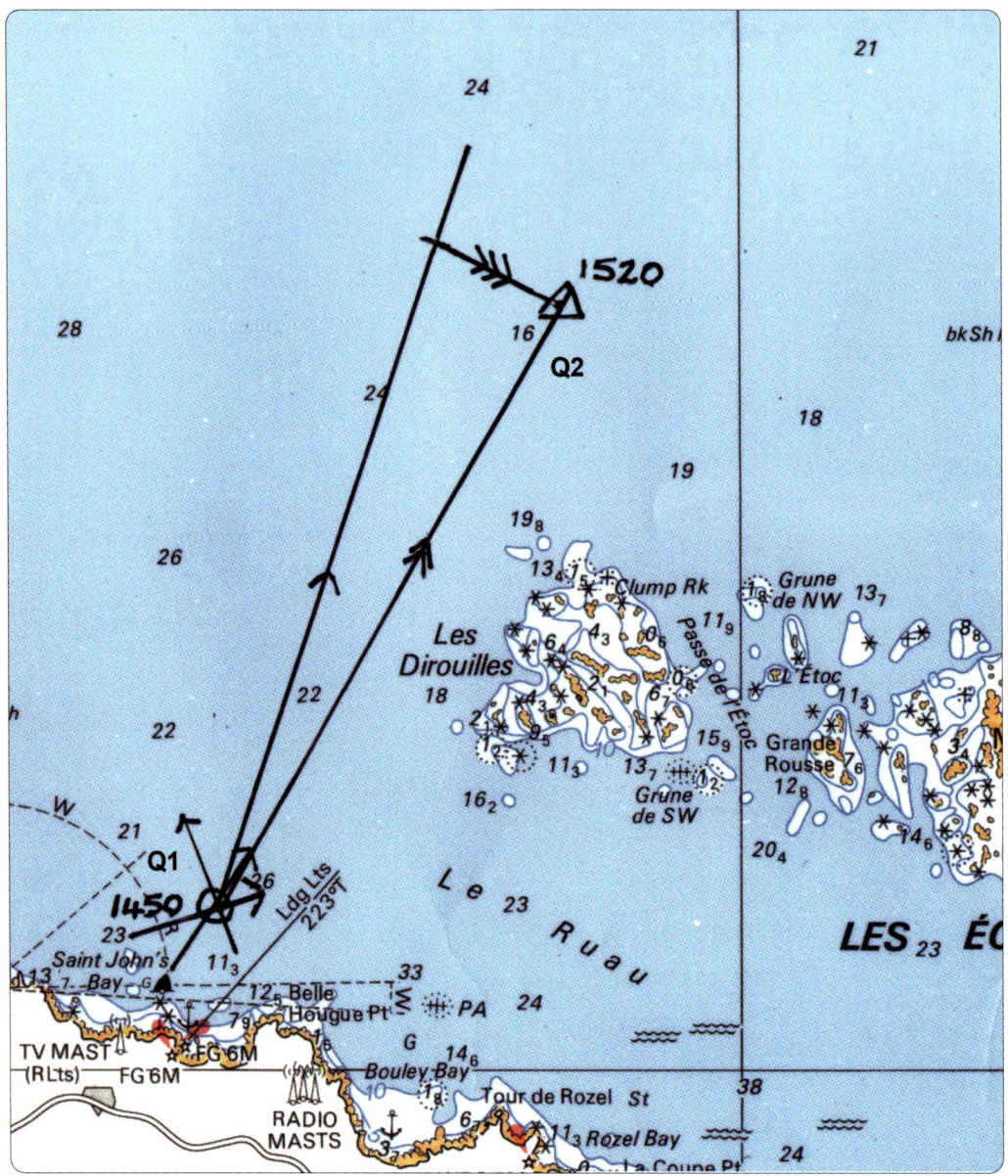

Fig A16.1 Q16.1 & 16.2.

ANSWERS • CHARTWORK TEST PAPER 2

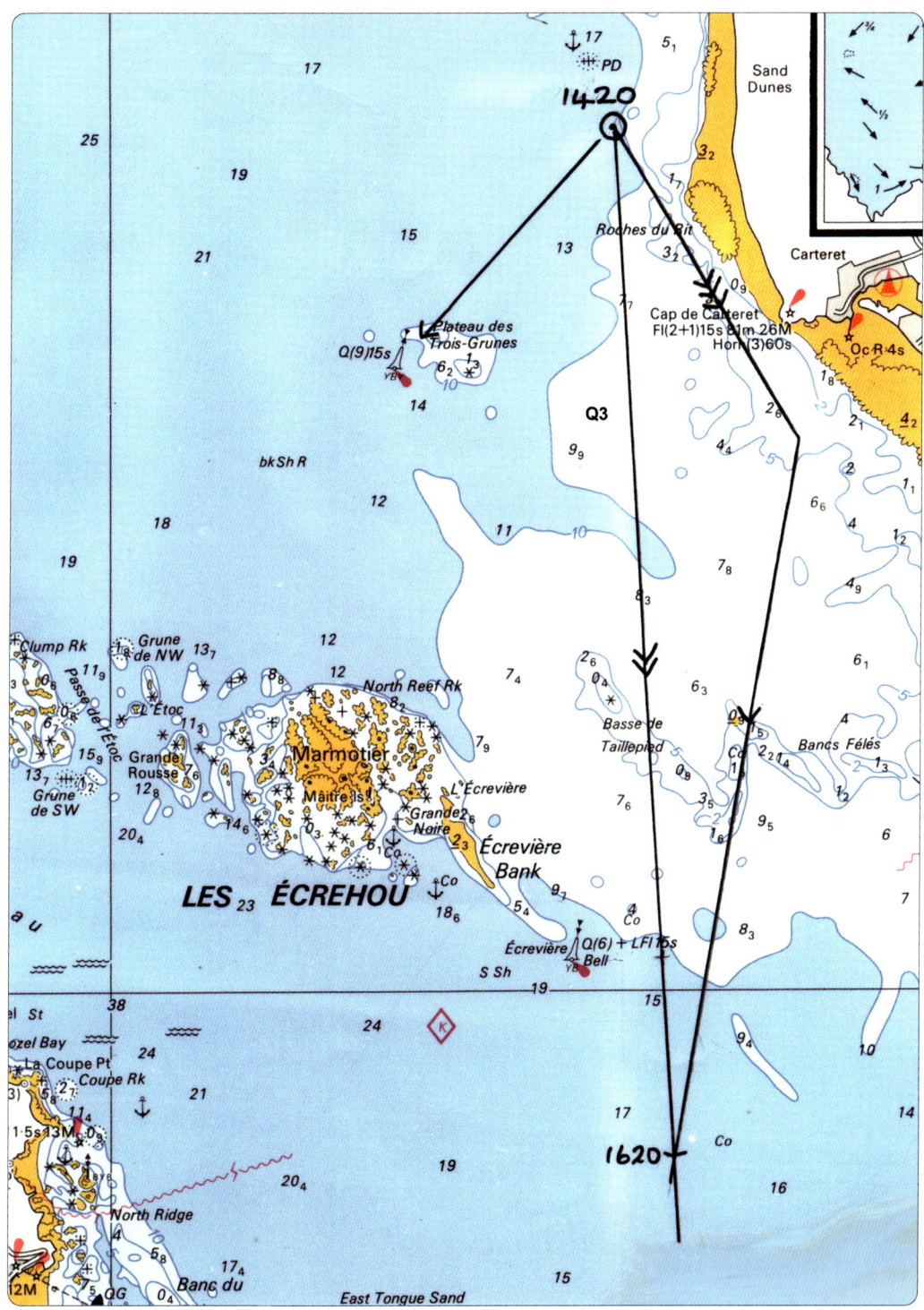

Fig A16.2 Q16.3.

87

16.4

14 November:

Range 10.0m (1st HW), 9.8m (2nd HW), springs.

St Helier UTC	HW 0712	11.3m	LW 1.3m	HW 1934	11.1m
Difference	+0007	0.0m	+0.1m	+0008	0.0m
St Catherine's UTC	0719	11.3m	1.4m	1942	11.1m

From St Helier curve, the height of tide at 0925 = 8.8m.

a) At 0925 the yacht is anchored in 3.0m water when the height of tide is 8.8m, so she must be anchored on a drying 5.8m beach as shown in Fig A16.3. The yacht draws 1.4m, which leaves 1.6m of water under the keel.
The tide has therefore to fall 1.6m for the yacht to ground.
Therefore the yacht grounds when the height of tide is 7.2m = 1010 UTC.

b) The tide has to fall a further 1.4m (the draught) for the yacht to dry out, ie to 5.8m.
The tidal height is 5.8m above chart datum at 1045 UTC.

c) Mark the new HW St Catherine's height (11.1m) on the HW line and the time of the next HW in the box at the bottom. Now calculate at what time the height of tide will rise to 7.2m when the yacht will refloat.

Answer = 1717 UTC.

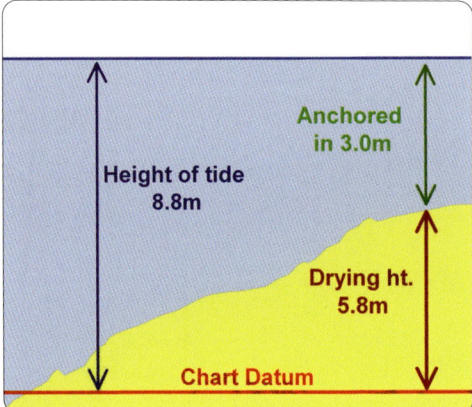

Fig A16.3 Tidal calculation for Q16.4.

EXTRACTS

All extracts are taken from *Reeds Nautical Almanac*.

EXTRACT 1: DOVER TIDETABLES – MAY TO AUGUST

TIME ZONE (UT) — For Summer Time add ONE hour in **non-shaded areas**

ENGLAND – DOVER
LAT 51°07′N LONG 1°19′E
TIMES AND HEIGHTS OF HIGH AND LOW WATERS

SPRING & NEAP TIDES
Dates in red are SPRINGS
Dates in blue are NEAPS

MAY

Day	Time	m	Time	m
1 SA	0300 / 0824 / 1530 / 2042	1.7 / 5.7 / 1.7 / 6.0		
16 SU	0426 / 0939 / 1642 / 2146	1.2 / 6.0 / 1.3 / 6.2		
2 SU	0353 / 0908 / 1620 / 2124	1.3 / 6.1 / 1.4 / 6.4		
17 M	0513 / 1014 / 1725 / 2225	1.1 / 6.2 / 1.2 / 6.4		
3 M	0443 / 0947 / 1708 / 2204	1.0 / 6.4 / 1.1 / 6.7		
18 TU	0552 / 1048 / 1802 / 2302	1.1 / 6.3 / 1.2 / 6.4		
4 TU ○	0533 / 1026 / 1754 / 2244	0.8 / 6.6 / 0.9 / 6.9		
19 W ●	0623 / 1121 / 1833 / 2336	1.1 / 6.3 / 1.2 / 6.4		
5 W	0620 / 1105 / 1838 / 2324	0.7 / 6.8 / 0.8 / 7.0		
20 TH	0650 / 1155 / 1900	1.2 / 6.3 / 1.2		
6 TH	0704 / 1146 / 1920	0.6 / 6.8 / 0.7		
21 F	0009 / 0714 / 1228 / 1926	6.3 / 1.3 / 6.3 / 1.2		
7 F	0007 / 0746 / 1230 / 2001	7.0 / 0.7 / 6.8 / 0.8		
22 SA	0038 / 0740 / 1258 / 1955	6.2 / 1.3 / 6.2 / 1.3		
8 SA	0053 / 0827 / 1318 / 2045	6.8 / 0.8 / 6.6 / 1.0		
23 SU	0104 / 0810 / 1325 / 2028	6.0 / 1.5 / 6.1 / 1.5		
9 SU	0143 / 0911 / 1412 / 2134	6.5 / 1.1 / 6.3 / 1.3		
24 M	0131 / 0843 / 1354 / 2104	5.9 / 1.6 / 5.9 / 1.7		
10 M	0243 / 1002 / 1513 / 2231	6.1 / 1.5 / 6.0 / 1.6		
25 TU	0207 / 0922 / 1436 / 2147	5.7 / 1.8 / 5.7 / 1.9		
11 TU ◐	0353 / 1105 / 1622 / 2343	5.7 / 1.9 / 5.7 / 1.8		
26 W	0258 / 1007 / 1533 / 2239	5.5 / 2.0 / 5.5 / 2.0		
12 W	0514 / 1223 / 1738	5.4 / 2.1 / 5.5		
27 TH ◐	0416 / 1104 / 1647 / 2350	5.3 / 2.2 / 5.4 / 2.1		
13 TH	0103 / 0648 / 1340 / 1904	1.9 / 5.4 / 2.0 / 5.5		
28 F	0538 / 1225 / 1800	5.3 / 2.2 / 5.4		
14 F	0220 / 0804 / 1555 / 2013	1.7 / 5.6 / 1.8 / 5.8		
29 SA	0109 / 0644 / 1342 / 1903	1.9 / 5.4 / 2.1 / 5.7		
15 SA	0328 / 0857 / 1551 / 2104	1.4 / 5.8 / 1.5 / 6.0		
30 SU	0214 / 0740 / 1443 / 1957	1.7 / 5.7 / 1.7 / 6.0		
			31 M	0310 / 0828 / 1539 / 2045	1.4 / 6.0 / 1.5 / 6.3

JUNE

Day	Time	m	Time	m
1 TU	0406 / 0914 / 1633 / 2132	1.1 / 6.3 / 1.2 / 6.6		
16 W	0509 / 1019 / 1726 / 2236	1.4 / 6.0 / 1.4 / 6.1		
2 W	0501 / 0958 / 1726 / 2218	0.9 / 6.5 / 1.0 / 6.7		
17 TH ●	0546 / 1057 / 1802 / 2314	1.4 / 6.1 / 1.2 / 6.1		
3 TH ○	0555 / 1045 / 1817 / 2306	0.8 / 6.6 / 0.9 / 6.8		
18 F	0618 / 1134 / 1835 / 2348	1.4 / 6.2 / 1.3 / 6.1		
4 F	0646 / 1132 / 1906 / 2355	0.8 / 6.7 / 0.9 / 6.8		
19 SA	0650 / 1209 / 1908	1.4 / 6.2 / 1.3		
5 SA	0736 / 1222 / 1956	0.8 / 6.7 / 0.9		
20 SU	0021 / 0722 / 1242 / 1942	6.1 / 1.4 / 6.2 / 1.4		
6 SU	0046 / 0824 / 1314 / 2046	6.6 / 1.0 / 6.6 / 0.9		
21 M	0053 / 0757 / 1313 / 2018	6.0 / 1.5 / 6.1 / 1.4		
7 M	0142 / 0914 / 1407 / 2139	6.4 / 1.1 / 6.4 / 1.1		
22 TU	0124 / 0833 / 1344 / 2057	5.9 / 1.6 / 6.1 / 1.5		
8 TU	0241 / 1006 / 1503 / 2234	6.2 / 1.4 / 6.2 / 1.3		
23 W	0158 / 0912 / 1421 / 2137	5.9 / 1.6 / 6.0 / 1.6		
9 W ◐	0343 / 1101 / 1601 / 2333	5.9 / 1.6 / 6.0 / 1.5		
24 TH	0238 / 0952 / 1505 / 2222	5.8 / 1.8 / 5.9 / 1.7		
10 TH	0449 / 1159 / 1703	5.6 / 1.8 / 5.8		
25 F ◐	0328 / 1038 / 1558 / 2314	5.7 / 1.9 / 5.8 / 1.7		
11 F	0034 / 0602 / 1300 / 1812	1.6 / 5.5 / 1.9 / 5.7		
26 SA	0429 / 1133 / 1700	5.6 / 2.2 / 5.7		
12 SA	0135 / 0712 / 1400 / 1922	1.6 / 5.5 / 1.9 / 5.7		
27 SU	0016 / 0541 / 1242 / 1807	1.8 / 5.6 / 2.0 / 5.8		
13 SU	0235 / 0810 / 1459 / 2021	1.6 / 5.6 / 1.8 / 5.9		
28 M	0124 / 0651 / 1353 / 1913	1.7 / 5.7 / 1.9 / 5.9		
14 M	0334 / 0857 / 1500 / 2111	1.6 / 5.7 / 1.7 / 5.9		
29 TU	0229 / 0752 / 1500 / 2013	1.5 / 5.8 / 1.7 / 6.1		
15 TU	0426 / 0940 / 1644 / 2156	1.5 / 5.9 / 1.5 / 6.0		
30 W	0333 / 0849 / 1604 / 2110	1.4 / 6.1 / 1.5 / 6.3		

JULY

Day	Time	m	Time	m
1 TH	0437 / 0943 / 1706 / 2206	1.2 / 6.3 / 1.2 / 6.5		
16 F	0514 / 1037 / 1737 / 2255	1.6 / 6.0 / 1.5 / 6.0		
2 F ○	0539 / 1037 / 1805 / 2301	0.9 / 6.5 / 1.0 / 6.6		
17 SA ●	0554 / 1115 / 1815 / 2330	1.5 / 6.2 / 1.4 / 6.1		
3 SA	0638 / 1129 / 1901 / 2355	0.9 / 6.6 / 0.9 / 6.6		
18 SU	0632 / 1149 / 1853	1.4 / 6.3 / 1.3		
4 SU	0734 / 1219 / 1956	0.9 / 6.7 / 0.8		
19 M	0003 / 0709 / 1222 / 1930	6.1 / 1.4 / 6.3 / 1.3		
5 M	0046 / 0825 / 1307 / 2047	6.6 / 0.9 / 6.7 / 0.8		
20 TU	0036 / 0747 / 1254 / 2009	6.1 / 1.4 / 6.3 / 1.2		
6 TU	0138 / 0912 / 1355 / 2135	6.4 / 1.0 / 6.6 / 0.8		
21 W	0107 / 0823 / 1325 / 2046	6.1 / 1.4 / 6.3 / 1.3		
7 W	0228 / 0956 / 1443 / 2221	6.3 / 1.1 / 6.5 / 1.0		
22 TH	0137 / 0859 / 1358 / 2123	6.1 / 1.4 / 6.3 / 1.3		
8 TH	0318 / 1038 / 1532 / 2305	6.1 / 1.3 / 6.3 / 1.2		
23 F	0212 / 0934 / 1437 / 2159	6.1 / 1.5 / 6.3 / 1.4		
9 F ◐	0410 / 1121 / 1623 / 2351	5.8 / 1.6 / 6.0 / 1.5		
24 SA	0253 / 1011 / 1521 / 2241	6.0 / 1.6 / 6.2 / 1.5		
10 SA	0505 / 1208 / 1720	5.6 / 1.8 / 5.7		
25 SU ◐	0342 / 1056 / 1615 / 2331	5.9 / 1.7 / 6.0 / 1.7		
11 SU	0042 / 0607 / 1303 / 1823	1.7 / 5.4 / 2.0 / 5.6		
26 M	0444 / 1153 / 1722	5.7 / 1.9 / 5.8		
12 M	0138 / 0713 / 1404 / 1932	1.8 / 5.3 / 2.1 / 5.5		
27 TU	0037 / 0606 / 1310 / 1840	1.8 / 5.5 / 2.1 / 5.7		
13 TU	0238 / 0814 / 1507 / 2035	1.8 / 5.4 / 2.0 / 5.6		
28 W	0155 / 0730 / 1431 / 1958	1.8 / 5.6 / 2.0 / 5.8		
14 W	0337 / 0908 / 1547 / 2130	1.9 / 5.6 / 1.7 / 5.7		
29 TH	0311 / 0841 / 1547 / 2109	1.7 / 5.8 / 1.7 / 6.0		
15 TH	0430 / 0956 / 1655 / 2216	1.7 / 5.8 / 1.6 / 5.9		
30 F	0425 / 0943 / 1657 / 2212	1.5 / 6.1 / 1.4 / 6.3		
			31 SA ○	0534 / 1038 / 1801 / 2308	1.2 / 6.3 / 1.1 / 6.5

AUGUST

Day	Time	m	Time	m
1 SU	0635 / 1126 / 1859 / 2357	1.0 / 6.6 / 0.8 / 6.6		
16 M ●	0615 / 1125 / 1836 / 2340	1.4 / 6.4 / 1.2 / 6.3		
2 M	0729 / 1211 / 1951	0.9 / 6.8 / 0.6		
17 TU	0654 / 1156 / 1915	1.3 / 6.5 / 1.1		
3 TU	0041 / 0815 / 1254 / 2037	6.6 / 0.8 / 6.8 / 0.6		
18 W	0011 / 0730 / 1228 / 1952	6.3 / 1.2 / 6.5 / 1.1		
4 TH	0123 / 0855 / 1335 / 2117	6.5 / 0.9 / 6.8 / 0.7		
19 TH	0041 / 0805 / 1259 / 2027	6.4 / 1.2 / 6.6 / 1.0		
5 TH	0203 / 0930 / 1417 / 2153	6.4 / 1.0 / 6.7 / 0.9		
20 F	0111 / 0838 / 1332 / 2100	6.4 / 1.2 / 6.6 / 1.1		
6 F	0243 / 1002 / 1458 / 2226	6.2 / 1.2 / 6.4 / 1.2		
21 SA	0144 / 0910 / 1408 / 2133	6.4 / 1.2 / 6.6 / 1.2		
7 SA ◐	0326 / 1033 / 1542 / 2300	5.9 / 1.5 / 6.1 / 1.5		
22 SU	0223 / 0944 / 1450 / 2210	6.2 / 1.4 / 6.4 / 1.4		
8 SU	0414 / 1107 / 1631 / 2341	5.6 / 1.9 / 5.8 / 1.8		
23 M ◐	0309 / 1026 / 1541 / 2257	6.0 / 1.7 / 6.1 / 1.8		
9 M	0512 / 1154 / 1731	5.3 / 2.2 / 5.4		
24 TU	0409 / 1121 / 1651	5.7 / 2.0 / 5.7		
10 TU	0037 / 0620 / 1307 / 1843	2.2 / 5.0 / 2.4 / 5.2		
25 W	0003 / 0543 / 1242 / 1830	2.1 / 5.3 / 2.3 / 5.4		
11 W	0150 / 0734 / 1426 / 2001	2.4 / 5.0 / 2.4 / 5.3		
26 TH	0136 / 0725 / 1418 / 2002	2.2 / 5.2 / 2.2 / 5.6		
12 TH	0300 / 0842 / 1534 / 2110	2.3 / 5.2 / 2.1 / 5.5		
27 F	0305 / 0841 / 1543 / 2118	2.0 / 5.7 / 1.8 / 5.9		
13 F	0400 / 0936 / 1629 / 2159	2.0 / 5.7 / 1.8 / 5.8		
28 SA	0426 / 0943 / 1657 / 2218	1.6 / 6.1 / 1.4 / 6.3		
14 SA	0451 / 1018 / 1715 / 2236	1.7 / 6.0 / 1.5 / 6.1		
29 SU	0532 / 1032 / 1758 / 2306	1.2 / 6.5 / 1.0 / 6.6		
15 SU	0535 / 1052 / 1756 / 2308	1.5 / 6.2 / 1.3 / 6.2		
30 M ○	0627 / 1115 / 1850 / 2346	1.0 / 6.8 / 0.7 / 6.7		
			31 TU	0713 / 1155 / 1935	0.8 / 6.9 / 0.5

YACHTMASTER EXERCISES FOR SAIL & POWER

EXTRACT 2: DOVER TIDETABLES – SEPTEMBER TO DECEMBER

TIME ZONE (UT)
For Summer Time add ONE hour in non-shaded areas

ENGLAND – DOVER
LAT 51°07'N   LONG 1°19'E
TIMES AND HEIGHTS OF HIGH AND LOW WATERS

SPRING & NEAP TIDES
Dates in red are SPRINGS
Dates in blue are NEAPS

SEPTEMBER

Day	Time m	Day	Time m
1	0023 6.7 / 0752 0.8 / W 1233 7.0 / 2014 0.6	**16**	0706 1.1 / 1157 6.8 / TH 1928 0.9
2	0057 6.6 / 0826 0.8 / TH 1310 6.9 / 2047 0.7	**17**	0012 6.6 / 0740 1.1 / F 1230 6.8 / 2002 0.9
3	0131 6.5 / 0855 1.0 / F 1346 6.7 / 2115 0.9	**18**	0043 6.7 / 0812 1.1 / SA 1304 6.8 / 2034 1.0
4	0206 6.3 / 0920 1.2 / SA 1422 6.5 / 2140 1.3	**19**	0118 6.6 / 0845 1.2 / SU 1341 6.7 / 2107 1.2
5	0243 6.0 / 0942 1.5 / SU 1458 6.1 / 2203 1.6	**20**	0158 6.4 / 0922 1.4 / M 1424 6.4 / 2146 1.5
6	0325 5.7 / 1009 1.9 / M 1542 5.7 / ◐ 2233 2.1	**21**	0246 6.1 / 1005 1.7 / TU 1519 5.9 / ◐ 2234 1.9
7	0422 5.3 / 1048 2.3 / TU 1645 5.3 / 2321 2.5	**22**	0352 5.6 / 1103 2.2 / W 1645 5.5 / 2345 2.4
8	0536 5.1 / 1154 2.6 / W 1804 5.0	**23**	0542 5.2 / 1233 2.4 / TH 1835 5.3
9	0101 2.7 / 0656 5.0 / TH 1349 2.6 / 1927 5.1	**24**	0132 2.4 / 0719 5.3 / F 1418 2.2 / 2008 5.6
10	0230 2.5 / 0813 5.3 / F 1506 2.3 / 2045 5.4	**25**	0309 2.1 / 0836 5.8 / SA 1546 1.7 / 2118 6.0
11	0335 2.1 / 0910 5.7 / SA 1603 1.9 / 2133 5.7	**26**	0424 1.6 / 0932 6.2 / SU 1652 1.2 / 2209 6.4
12	0427 1.8 / 0949 6.0 / SU 1649 1.5 / 2207 6.1	**27**	0520 1.2 / 1016 6.6 / M 1745 0.9 / 2250 6.6
13	0512 1.5 / 1022 6.3 / M 1732 1.3 / 2238 6.3	**28**	0606 1.0 / 1055 6.8 / TU 1830 0.7 / ○ 2324 6.7
14	0552 1.3 / 1054 6.5 / TU 1812 1.1 / ● 2310 6.4	**29**	0647 0.9 / 1132 7.0 / W 1910 0.6 / 2356 6.7
15	0630 1.2 / 1126 6.7 / W 1851 1.0 / 2341 6.5	**30**	0721 0.9 / 1207 7.0 / TH 1943 0.7

OCTOBER

Day	Time m	Day	Time m
1	0028 6.7 / 0750 1.0 / F 1242 6.9 / 2010 0.9	**16**	0713 1.0 / 1201 7.0 / SA 1936 0.9
2	0100 6.6 / 0815 1.1 / SA 1315 6.7 / 2032 1.2	**17**	0018 6.8 / 0749 1.0 / SU 1239 6.9 / 2011 1.0
3	0132 6.4 / 0836 1.3 / SU 1345 6.4 / 2052 1.4	**18**	0057 6.7 / 0826 1.2 / M 1321 6.6 / 2048 1.3
4	0203 6.1 / 0858 1.6 / M 1415 6.1 / 2115 1.7	**19**	0142 6.4 / 0907 1.4 / TU 1410 6.3 / 2130 1.6
5	0235 5.8 / 0928 1.9 / TU 1450 5.7 / 2148 2.1	**20**	0238 6.0 / 0955 1.8 / W 1517 5.8 / ◐ 2224 2.1
6	0325 5.5 / 1008 2.3 / W 1602 5.2 / ◐ 2232 2.6	**21**	0357 5.5 / 1100 2.2 / TH 1652 5.4 / 2344 2.4
7	0455 5.1 / 1104 2.6 / TH 1731 5.0 / 2348 2.8	**22**	0531 5.4 / 1236 2.3 / F 1831 5.4
8	0616 5.0 / 1302 2.8 / F 1851 5.0	**23**	0129 2.4 / 0703 5.5 / SA 1414 2.0 / 1959 5.6
9	0154 2.7 / 0731 5.2 / SA 1429 2.4 / 2002 5.3	**24**	0256 2.0 / 0816 5.9 / SU 1531 1.6 / 2101 6.0
10	0303 2.3 / 0909 6.3 / SU 1527 1.9 / 2051 5.7	**25**	0401 1.6 / 0909 6.3 / M 1631 1.2 / 2146 6.3
11	0355 1.9 / 0909 6.0 / M 1614 1.5 / 2129 6.1	**26**	0453 1.2 / 0951 6.6 / TU 1720 0.9 / 2224 6.5
12	0439 1.6 / 0944 6.3 / TU 1658 1.2 / 2203 6.4	**27**	0536 1.1 / 1029 6.7 / W 1802 0.8 / 2256 6.6
13	0520 1.3 / 1018 6.6 / W 1741 1.0 / 2236 6.6	**28**	0614 1.0 / 1106 6.8 / TH 1837 0.9 / ○ 2327 6.6
14	0600 1.2 / 1051 6.8 / TH 1821 0.9 / ● 2309 6.7	**29**	0646 1.0 / 1141 6.8 / F 1907 1.0
15	0637 1.1 / 1126 6.9 / F 1859 0.9 / 2342 6.8	**30**	0000 6.6 / 0714 1.1 / SA 1215 6.7 / 1931 1.2
		31	0033 6.5 / 0738 1.3 / SU 1246 6.5 / 1952 1.3

NOVEMBER

Day	Time m	Day	Time m
1	0104 6.4 / 0801 1.4 / M 1314 6.3 / 2014 1.5	**16**	0046 6.7 / 0816 1.1 / TU 1311 6.6 / 2039 1.3
2	0133 6.2 / 0828 1.6 / TU 1341 6.0 / 2043 1.8	**17**	0138 6.5 / 0903 1.4 / W 1409 6.2 / 2128 1.6
3	0201 5.9 / 0902 1.9 / W 1414 5.7 / 2119 2.1	**18**	0240 6.1 / 0959 1.7 / TH 1521 5.9 / 2227 2.0
4	0239 5.6 / 0943 2.2 / TH 1515 5.3 / 2204 2.4	**19**	0350 5.9 / 1108 1.9 / F 1643 5.6 / ◐ 2343 2.2
5	0403 5.3 / 1036 2.5 / F 1653 5.0 / 2304 2.7	**20**	0506 5.7 / 1227 2.0 / SA 1810 5.5
6	0527 5.1 / 1202 2.6 / SA 1808 5.1	**21**	0103 2.2 / 0627 5.7 / SU 1345 1.8 / 1927 5.6
7	0055 2.7 / 0638 5.3 / SU 1337 2.4 / 1913 5.3	**22**	0216 2.0 / 0739 5.9 / M 1455 1.6 / 2027 5.9
8	0214 2.4 / 0736 5.6 / M 1439 2.0 / 2005 5.7	**23**	0320 1.7 / 0834 6.1 / TU 1555 1.3 / 2113 6.1
9	0310 2.0 / 0822 5.9 / TU 1531 1.6 / 2048 6.0	**24**	0414 1.5 / 0920 6.3 / W 1646 1.2 / 2152 6.2
10	0359 1.7 / 0902 6.3 / W 1620 1.3 / 2125 6.3	**25**	0500 1.4 / 1001 6.5 / TH 1728 1.2 / 2227 6.3
11	0444 1.4 / 0940 6.6 / TH 1706 1.1 / 2202 6.6	**26**	0540 1.2 / 1040 6.5 / F 1803 1.2 / ○ 2301 6.4
12	0528 1.2 / 1018 6.8 / F 1751 0.9 / ● 2239 6.7	**27**	0614 1.2 / 1116 6.5 / SA 1832 1.3 / 2336 6.5
13	0610 1.1 / 1057 6.9 / SA 1834 0.9 / 2318 6.8	**28**	0645 1.3 / 1151 6.4 / SU 1859 1.5
14	0651 1.0 / 1138 7.0 / SU 1915 0.9	**29**	0011 6.4 / 0712 1.4 / M 1225 6.3 / 1924 1.5
15	0000 6.8 / 0732 1.0 / M 1223 6.8 / 1955 1.1	**30**	0045 6.3 / 0740 1.5 / TU 1256 6.1 / 1952 1.6

DECEMBER

Day	Time m	Day	Time m
1	0116 6.2 / 0811 1.6 / W 1325 5.9 / 2025 1.7	**16**	0137 6.6 / 0911 1.1 / TH 1408 6.3 / 2134 1.4
2	0145 6.0 / 0847 1.8 / TH 1358 5.7 / 2102 1.9	**17**	0232 6.4 / 1005 1.3 / F 1510 6.1 / 2227 1.6
3	0220 5.8 / 0928 1.9 / F 1442 5.5 / 2145 2.1	**18**	0330 6.2 / 1101 1.4 / SA 1615 5.8 / ◐ 2322 1.8
4	0308 5.6 / 1016 2.1 / SA 1547 5.3 / 2235 2.3	**19**	0431 6.0 / 1159 1.6 / SU 1724 5.6
5	0415 5.4 / 1117 2.2 / SU 1708 5.2 / ◐ 2341 2.4	**20**	0021 1.9 / 0537 5.8 / M 1259 1.7 / 1834 5.5
6	0529 5.4 / 1233 2.2 / M 1817 5.3	**21**	0122 2.0 / 0647 5.8 / TU 1400 1.7 / 1937 5.6
7	0105 2.4 / 0635 5.6 / TU 1343 2.0 / 1915 5.6	**22**	0225 2.0 / 0751 5.8 / W 1502 1.7 / 2032 5.7
8	0214 2.1 / 0731 5.8 / W 1443 1.7 / 2004 5.8	**23**	0326 1.9 / 0846 5.9 / TH 1601 1.6 / 2119 5.8
9	0313 1.8 / 0819 6.1 / TH 1539 1.4 / 2049 6.1	**24**	0422 1.7 / 0935 6.0 / F 1651 1.6 / 2202 6.0
10	0407 1.6 / 0905 6.4 / F 1633 1.2 / 2133 6.4	**25**	0508 1.6 / 1019 6.1 / SA 1730 1.5 / 2241 6.2
11	0459 1.3 / 0951 6.6 / SA 1726 1.0 / 2218 6.6	**26**	0548 1.5 / 1058 6.1 / SU 1805 1.5 / ○ 2319 6.3
12	0549 1.1 / 1038 6.8 / SU 1815 1.0 / ● 2305 6.7	**27**	0622 1.4 / 1135 6.2 / M 1836 1.5 / 2355 6.3
13	0638 1.0 / 1126 6.8 / M 1904 1.0 / 2353 6.8	**28**	0655 1.4 / 1209 6.2 / TU 1908 1.5
14	0727 1.0 / 1217 6.7 / TU 1953 1.0	**29**	0029 6.3 / 0727 1.4 / W 1242 6.1 / 1940 1.5
15	0043 6.7 / 0818 1.0 / W 1310 6.5 / 2043 1.2	**30**	0100 6.3 / 0802 1.5 / TH 1312 6.0 / 2015 1.6
		31	0129 6.2 / 0839 1.5 / F 1342 5.9 / 2051 1.7

EXTRACT 3: TIDAL STREAMS, BASED ON HW DOVER

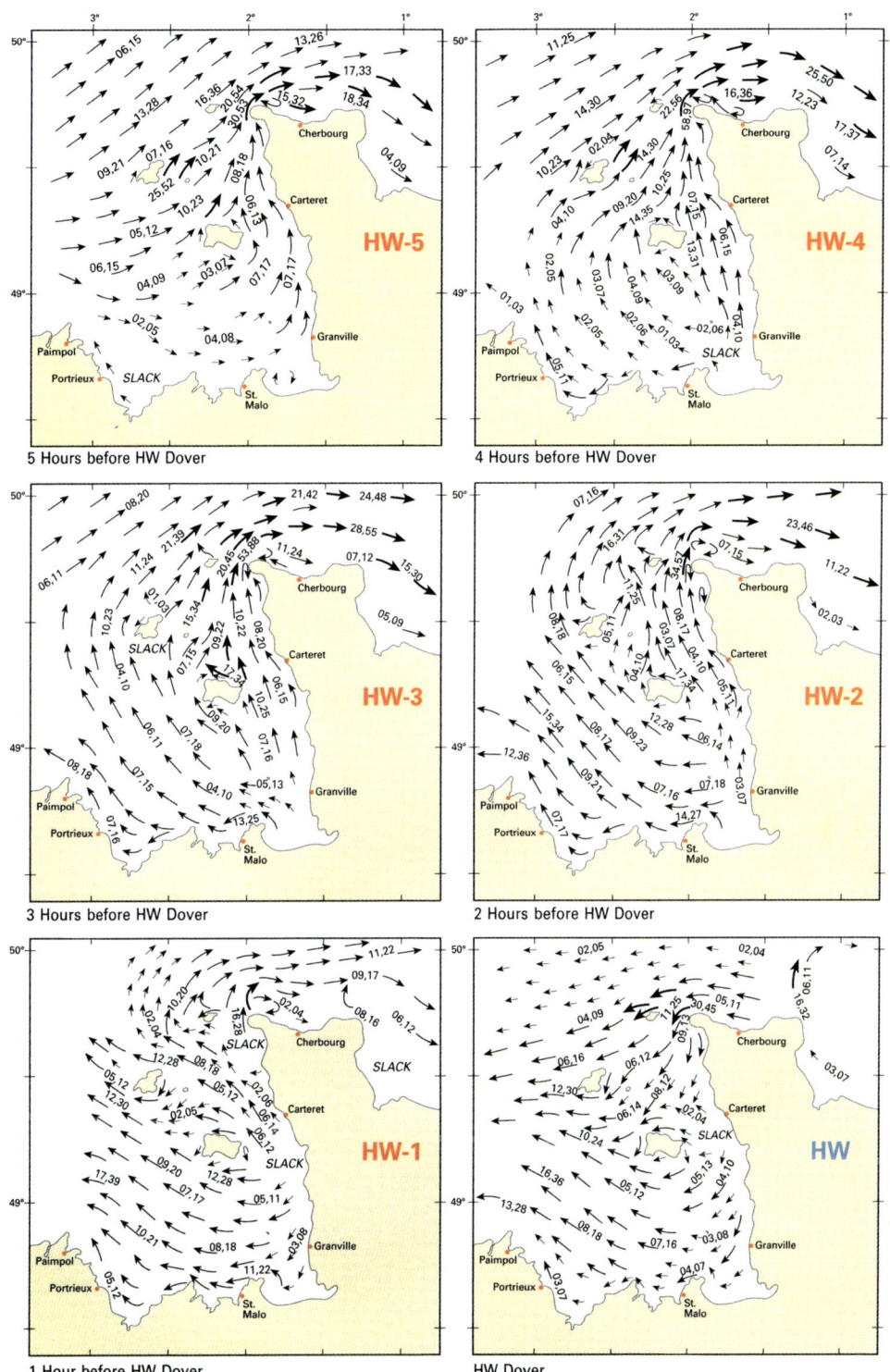

EXTRACT 4: TIDAL STREAMS, BASED ON HW DOVER (CONTINUED)

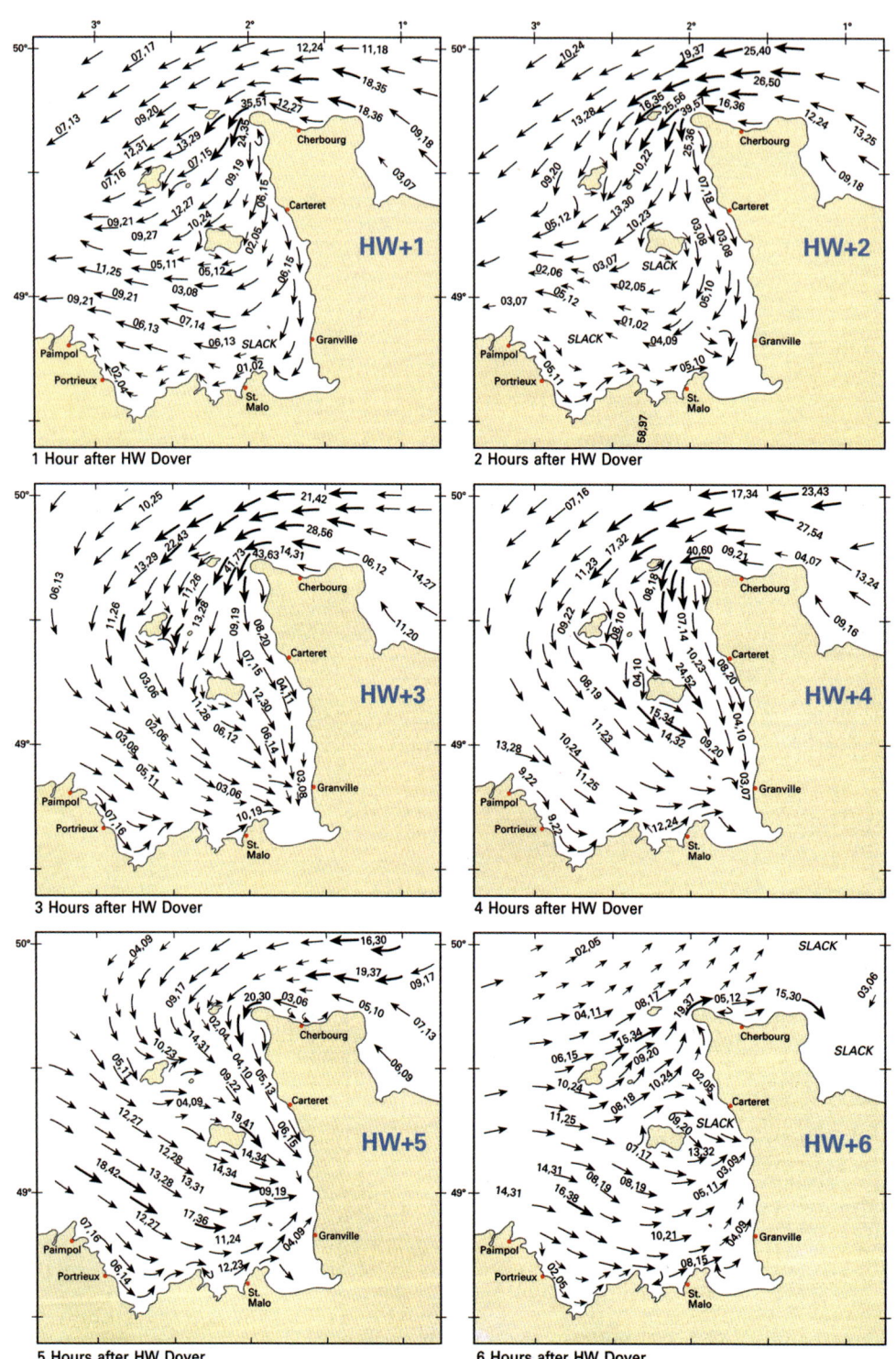

EXTRACTS

EXTRACT 5: ST HELIER TIDETABLE

CHANNEL ISLANDS – ST HELIER
LAT 49°11′N   LONG 2°07′W
TIMES AND HEIGHTS OF HIGH AND LOW WATERS

TIME ZONE (UT)
For Summer Time add ONE hour in **non-shaded areas**

SPRING & NEAP TIDES
Dates in red are SPRINGS
Dates in blue are NEAPS

SEPTEMBER

Day	Time m	Time m	Day	Time m	Time m
1	0222 0.7 / 0754 11.2	W 1437 1.0 / 2010 11.5	**16**	0152 1.3 / 0728 10.9	TH 1404 1.3 / 1940 11.2
2	0258 0.9 / 0828 11.0	TH 1510 1.3 / 2043 11.1	**17**	0225 1.2 / 0801 11.0	F 1438 1.3 / 2014 11.2
3	0329 1.3 / 0859 10.6	F 1539 1.8 / 2114 10.5	**18**	0258 1.4 / 0834 10.8	SA 1512 1.6 / 2049 10.8
4	0355 2.0 / 0927 10.0	SA 1605 2.4 / 2142 9.7	**19**	0330 1.8 / 0908 10.4	SU 1546 2.0 / 2123 10.2
5	0419 2.7 / 0954 9.4	SU 1630 3.1 / 2210 8.9	**20**	0403 2.4 / 0942 9.8	M 1623 2.7 / 2202 9.5
6	0444 3.4 / 1023 8.7	M 1659 3.8 / 2244 8.1	**21**	0441 3.1 / 1023 9.0	TU 1710 3.4 / 2252 8.6
7	0518 4.2 / 1104 7.9	TU 1747 4.5 / 2341 7.4	**22**	0534 3.9 / 1125 8.3	W 1821 4.0
8	0620 4.8 / 1224 7.3	W 1916 4.9	**23**	0016 7.9 / 0704 4.4	TH 1315 7.9 / 2007 4.1
9	0153 7.1 / 0807 4.9	TH 1434 7.4 / 2111 4.6	**24**	0222 7.9 / 0858 4.1	F 1505 8.5 / 2144 3.4
10	0330 7.6 / 0946 4.4	F 1549 8.1 / 2224 3.9	**25**	0349 8.7 / 1020 3.3	SA 1613 9.4 / 2252 2.5
11	0425 8.3 / 1045 3.7	SA 1637 8.8 / 2314 3.1	**26**	0446 9.7 / 1119 2.3	SU 1705 10.3 / 2346 1.7
12	0507 9.1 / 1131 2.9	SU 1718 9.6 / 2357 2.4	**27**	0532 10.4 / 1208 1.6	M 1749 11.0
13	0544 9.7 / 1213 2.3	M 1755 10.2	**28**	0033 1.1 / 0613 11.0	TU 1253 1.2 / 1829 11.4
14	0037 1.9 / 0619 10.2	TU 1252 1.8 / 1830 10.7	**29**	0115 0.9 / 0651 11.2	W 1331 1.1 / 1906 11.5
15	0116 1.5 / 0654 10.6	W 1329 1.5 / 1905 11.0	**30**	0151 0.9 / 0724 11.2	TH 1405 1.2 / 1940 11.3

OCTOBER

Day	Time m	Time m	Day	Time m	Time m
1	0222 1.2 / 0755 11.1	F 1435 1.5 / 2010 10.9	**16**	0159 1.2 / 0735 11.2	SA 1415 1.2 / 1952 11.3
2	0249 1.6 / 0823 10.6	SA 1501 1.9 / 2038 10.4	**17**	0234 1.4 / 0811 11.0	SU 1452 1.5 / 2029 10.9
3	0313 2.1 / 0848 10.1	SU 1525 2.5 / 2104 9.7	**18**	0309 1.8 / 0847 10.6	M 1530 2.0 / 2108 10.2
4	0336 2.8 / 0912 9.5	M 1549 3.1 / 2129 8.8	**19**	0347 2.5 / 0926 9.9	TU 1612 2.7 / 2153 9.3
5	0400 3.5 / 0938 8.8	TU 1617 3.9 / 2157 8.1	**20**	0430 3.3 / 1014 9.1	W 1706 3.4 / 2252 8.5
6	0432 4.3 / 1010 8.1	W 1700 4.5 / 2244 7.4	**21**	0532 4.1 / 1126 8.3	TH 1825 4.0
7	0528 4.9 / 1115 7.3	TH 1824 5.0	**22**	0026 7.9 / 0708 4.4	F 1317 8.2 / 2007 3.9
8	0105 7.0 / 0714 5.2	F 1352 7.2 / 2026 4.8	**23**	0217 8.2 / 0850 4.0	SA 1450 8.7 / 2130 3.2
9	0258 7.5 / 0907 4.7	SA 1515 7.9 / 2148 4.1	**24**	0330 8.9 / 1001 3.1	SU 1552 9.5 / 2230 2.4
10	0352 8.3 / 1011 3.8	SU 1604 8.8 / 2239 3.2	**25**	0422 9.7 / 1055 2.4	M 1641 10.2 / 2320 1.8
11	0433 9.1 / 1057 3.0	M 1644 9.6 / 2322 2.5	**26**	0506 10.3 / 1142 1.8	TU 1723 10.7
12	0511 9.8 / 1140 2.3	TU 1723 10.3	**27**	0004 1.5 / 0544 10.7	W 1223 1.6 / 1801 10.9
13	0004 1.9 / 0547 10.4	W 1221 1.8 / 1800 10.8	**28**	0042 1.4 / 0620 10.9	TH 1259 1.5 / 1837 11.0
14	0044 1.4 / 0623 10.9	TH 1301 1.4 / 1837 11.2	**29**	0116 1.5 / 0652 10.9	F 1331 1.6 / 1910 10.8
15	0123 1.2 / 0659 11.2	F 1339 1.2 / 1914 11.3	**30**	0145 1.7 / 0722 10.8	SA 1400 1.9 / 1940 10.6
31	0212 2.0 / 0750 10.5	SU 1427 2.1 / 2008 10.1			

NOVEMBER

Day	Time m	Time m	Day	Time m	Time m
1	0238 2.4 / 0816 10.1	M 1453 2.6 / 2035 9.6	**16**	0257 1.9 / 0837 10.7	TU 1523 1.9 / 2104 10.1
2	0305 2.9 / 0842 9.6	TU 1521 3.1 / 2103 8.9	**17**	0341 2.5 / 0923 10.0	W 1612 2.5 / 2155 9.4
3	0332 3.5 / 0910 9.0	W 1552 3.7 / 2134 8.3	**18**	0432 3.2 / 1017 9.4	TH 1710 3.1 / 2257 8.8
4	0406 4.2 / 0944 8.3	TH 1635 4.3 / 2220 7.6	**19**	0536 3.7 / 1126 8.8	F 1823 3.5
5	0458 4.7 / 1041 7.7	F 1744 4.7 / 2353 7.2	**20**	0015 8.4 / 0656 4.0	SA 1251 8.6 / 1943 3.5
6	0622 5.0 / 1231 7.4	SA 1921 4.7	**21**	0140 8.4 / 0817 3.7	SU 1411 8.8 / 2055 3.2
7	0152 7.5 / 0802 4.7	SU 1413 7.8 / 2049 4.2	**22**	0250 8.8 / 0925 3.3	M 1515 9.3 / 2154 2.7
8	0258 8.1 / 0918 4.0	M 1513 8.6 / 2149 3.4	**23**	0346 9.4 / 1021 2.8	TU 1608 9.7 / 2245 2.4
9	0347 8.9 / 1012 3.2	TU 1600 9.3 / 2239 2.7	**24**	0432 9.8 / 1109 2.4	W 1653 10.0 / 2329 2.2
10	0430 9.7 / 1100 2.5	W 1644 10.1 / 2325 2.1	**25**	0513 10.1 / 1151 2.2	TH 1733 10.2
11	0511 10.3 / 1145 1.9	TH 1727 10.7	**26**	0008 2.1 / 0549 10.3	F 1228 2.1 / 1810 10.3
12	0009 1.6 / 0551 10.8	F 1230 1.5 / 1809 11.1	**27**	0043 2.1 / 0623 10.4	SA 1302 2.1 / 1844 10.2
13	0053 1.4 / 0632 11.2	SA 1313 1.3 / 1851 11.2	**28**	0114 2.1 / 0656 10.4	SU 1333 2.2 / 1917 10.1
14	0134 1.3 / 0712 11.3	SU 1355 1.3 / 1934 11.1	**29**	0145 2.3 / 0726 10.3	M 1404 2.3 / 1949 9.8
15	0215 1.5 / 0754 11.1	M 1438 1.5 / 2018 10.7	**30**	0216 2.5 / 0757 10.0	TU 1435 2.6 / 2020 9.5

DECEMBER

Day	Time m	Time m	Day	Time m	Time m
1	0246 2.9 / 0827 9.6	W 1506 3.0 / 2052 9.1	**16**	0342 2.1 / 0923 10.5	TH 1614 2.0 / 2154 9.9
2	0318 3.3 / 0859 9.2	TH 1540 3.4 / 2127 8.6	**17**	0432 2.6 / 1013 10.0	F 1706 2.4 / 2245 9.4
3	0354 3.7 / 0936 8.8	F 1621 3.8 / 2210 8.2	**18**	0525 3.0 / 1107 9.5	SA 1801 2.9 / 2342 8.9
4	0439 4.1 / 1024 8.3	SA 1713 4.1 / 2308 7.9	**19**	0624 3.4 / 1208 9.0	SU 1901 3.2
5	0538 4.4 / 1130 8.0	SU 1820 4.2	**20**	0045 8.6 / 0728 3.6	M 1316 8.7 / 2003 3.4
6	0025 7.8 / 0652 4.6	M 1250 8.0 / 1936 4.1	**21**	0153 8.5 / 0834 3.6	TU 1424 8.7 / 2105 3.3
7	0144 8.1 / 0810 4.1	TU 1405 8.4 / 2048 3.7	**22**	0257 8.7 / 0937 3.4	W 1526 8.8 / 2203 3.2
8	0248 8.6 / 0918 3.5	W 1507 9.0 / 2150 3.1	**23**	0354 9.0 / 1033 3.2	TH 1621 9.1 / 2254 3.0
9	0343 9.3 / 1017 2.9	TH 1603 9.6 / 2245 2.5	**24**	0442 9.3 / 1122 2.8	F 1708 9.3 / 2339 2.8
10	0434 9.9 / 1111 2.3	F 1655 10.2 / 2337 2.0	**25**	0525 9.6 / 1204 2.7	SA 1750 9.5
11	0523 10.5 / 1203 1.8	SA 1746 10.6	**26**	0018 2.6 / 0603 9.9	SU 1242 2.5 / 1828 9.7
12	0028 1.7 / 0611 10.9	SU 1254 1.4 / 1836 10.9	**27**	0056 2.5 / 0639 10.0	M 1318 2.4 / 1905 9.8
13	0117 1.5 / 0658 11.1	M 1344 1.3 / 1926 10.9	**28**	0130 2.5 / 0713 10.0	TU 1352 2.4 / 1939 9.7
14	0206 1.6 / 0746 11.1	TU 1433 1.3 / 2015 10.8	**29**	0204 2.5 / 0747 10.0	W 1426 2.4 / 2012 9.6
15	0254 1.8 / 0834 10.9	W 1523 1.6 / 2104 10.4	**30**	0237 2.6 / 0819 9.9	TH 1459 2.6 / 2045 9.5
31	0309 2.8 / 0853 9.7	F 1532 2.8 / 2118 9.2			

Chart Datum: 5·88 metres below Ordnance Datum (Local)

EXTRACT 6: PORT INFORMATION FOR ST HELIER

ST HELIER

Standard Port ST HELIER

Times				Height (metres)			
High Water		Low Water		MHWS	MHWN	MLWN	MLWS
0300	0900	0200	0900	11·0	8·1	4·0	1·4
1500	2100	1400	2100				
Differences ST CATHERINE BAY							
0000	+0010	+0010	+0010	0·0	−0·1	0·0	+0·1
Differences BRAYE							
+0050	+0040	+0025	+0105	−4·8	−3·4	−1·5	−0·5

Jersey (Channel Is) 49°10'·57N 02°06'·98W ✴✴✴✴✴✴✴

CHARTS AC *3655, 1137,3278, 5604*; SHOM *7160, 7161, 6938*; ECM *534, 1014*; Imray *C33B*; Stanfords *16, 26*

TIDES –0455 Dover; ML 6·1; Duration 0545; Zone 0 (UT) NOTE: St Helier is a Standard Port. The tidal range is very large.

SHELTER Excellent. Visitors berth in **St Helier marina**, access HW±3 over sill (CD+3·6m); hinged gate rises 1·4m above sill to retain 5m. Digital gauge shows depth over sill. A waiting pontoon is to W of marina ent, near LB. Depths in marina vary from 2·8m at ent to 2·1m at N end. ♥ berths as directed by staff (yachts >12m LOA or >2·1m draft, use pontoon A). Good shelter in **La Collette basin**, 1·8m; access H24, to await the tide. Caution: Ent narrow at LWS; keep close to W side; PHM buoys mark shoal on E side. Waiting berths on pontoon D and W side of C. FVs berth on W of basin. **Elizabeth marina** is mainly for local boats; access HW±3 over sill/flap gate; max LOA 20m, drafts 2·1 – 3·5m. No ⚓ in St Helier Rds due to shipping & fish storage boxes.

NAVIGATION WPT 49°09'·95N 02°07'·38W, 023°/0·74M to front ldg lt. This WPT is common to all St Helier appr's:
1. W Passage (082°); beware race off Noirmont Pt, HW to HW +4.
1A. NW Passage (095°, much used by yachts) passes 6ca S of La Corbière lt ho to join W Passage abm Noirmont Pt.

LIGHTS AND MARKS Power stn chy (95m, floodlit) and W concave roofs of Fort Regent are conspic, close E of R & G ldg line. **W Passage** ldg lts: Front Oc 5s 23m 14M; rear Oc R 5s 46m 12M and Dog's Nest bn (unlit) lead 082°, N of Les Fours, NCM Q, and Ruaudière, SHM Fl G 3s, buoys, to a position close to E Rock, SHM buoy QG, where course is altered to pick up the **Red & Green Passage** ldg lts 023°: Front Oc G 5s; rear Oc R 5s, synch; (now easier to see against town lts) Daymarks are red dayglow patches on front dolphin and rear lt twr. Nos 2 and 4 PHM buoys (both QR) mark the fairway N of Platte Rk (Fl R 1·5s). Outer pier hds and dolphin are painted white and floodlit. Inner ldg lts 078°, both FG on W columns are not essential for yachts.

IPTS (Sigs 1-4) are shown from the base of the Port Control tower and are easily seen from Small Road, La Collette and the Main Hbr. Repeater lts are shown in conjunction from the top of the tower, during shipping and high-speed ferry movements. They are: L Fl R 5s with Sig 1; Oc R 8s with Sig 2; Oc G 8s with Sig 3; and Oc Y 4s with Sig 4. The Oc Y 4s is used whenever possible. It exempts power-driven craft <25m LOA from the main display signals. Keep to stbd, well clear of shipping, and keep a sharp all-round lookout. Monitor VHF Ch 14 during arr/dep.
Local IPTS control arr/dep to/from St Helier and Elizabeth marinas (but not La Collette), with large digital tide gauges showing depth over the sills.

R/T Monitor *St Helier Port Control* VHF Ch 14 (H24) for ferry/ shipping movements. No marina VHF, but call *Port Control* if essential. Do not use Ch M. If unable to pass messages to *Port Control*, these can be relayed via *Jersey Radio* CRS, Ch **82** 25 16 (H24) or ☎ 741121.

St Helier Pierheads broadcasts recorded wind info every 2 mins on VHF Ch 18. It consists of: wind direction, speed and gusts meaned over the last 2 minutes.

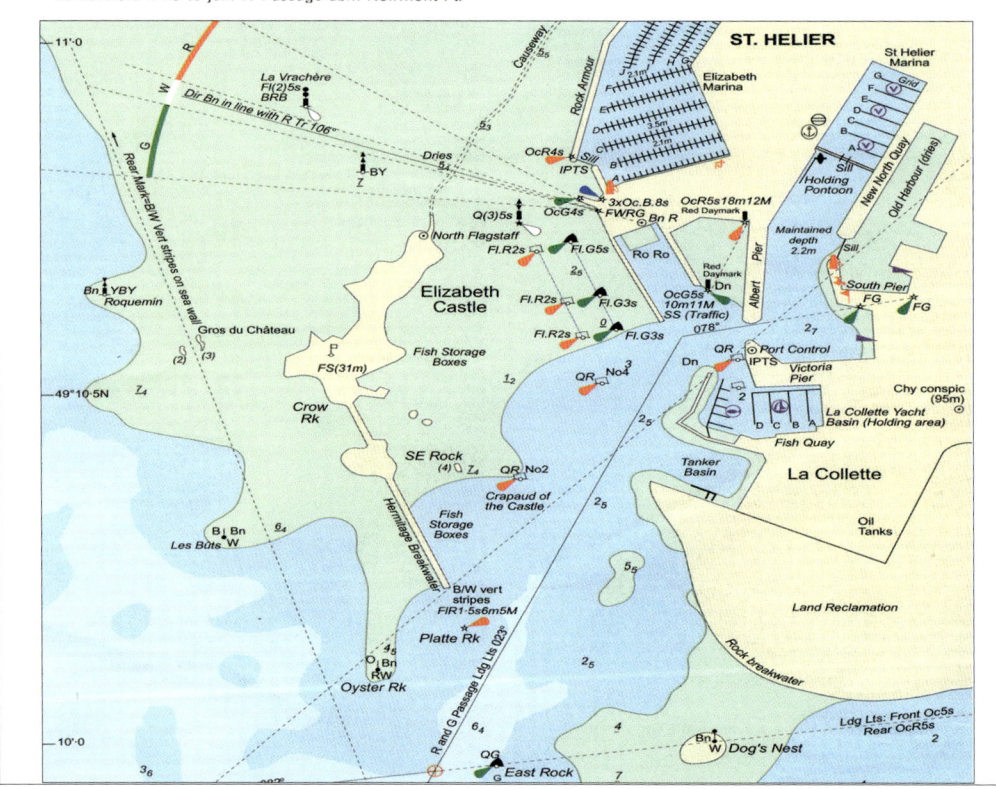

EXTRACTS

EXTRACT 7: ST HELIER TIDAL CURVE

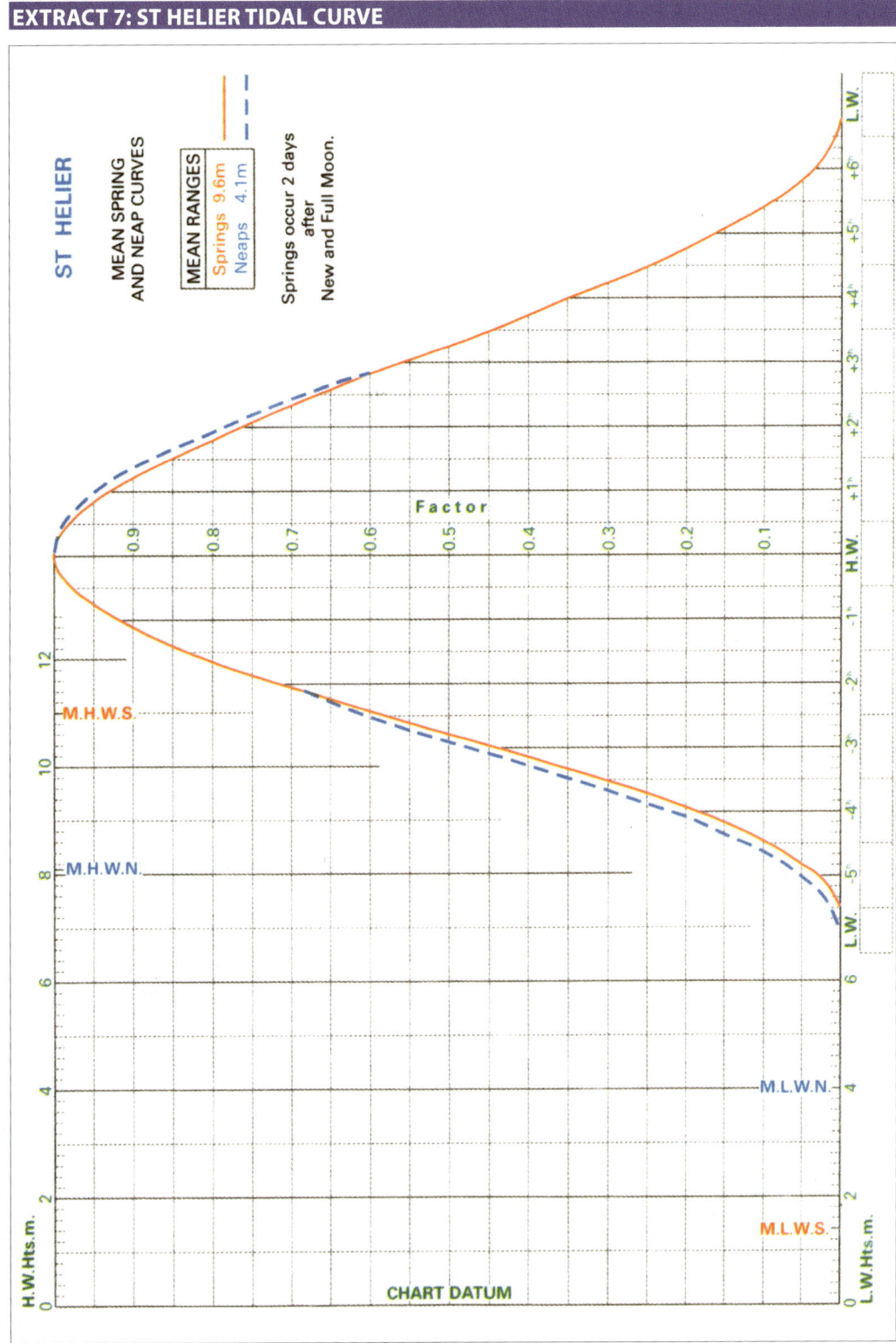

YACHTMASTER EXERCISES FOR SAIL & POWER

EXTRACT 8: CHERBOURG TIDAL CURVE

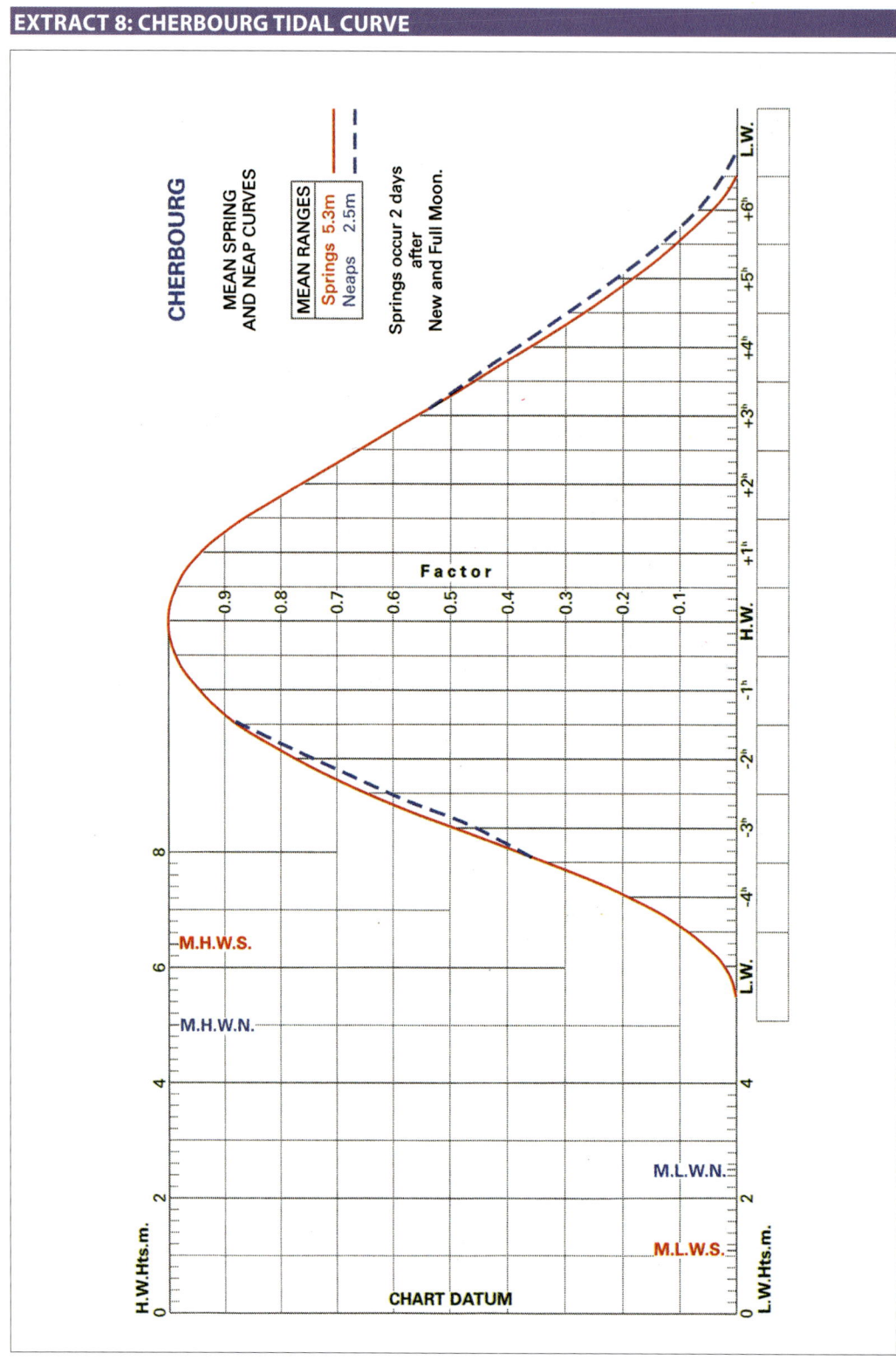

EXTRACT 9: CHERBOURG TIDETABLE

TIME ZONE -0100
(French Standard Time)
Subtract 1 hour for UT
For French Summer Time add
ONE hour in non-shaded areas

FRANCE – CHERBOURG
LAT 49°39′N   LONG 1°38′W
TIMES AND HEIGHTS OF HIGH AND LOW WATERS

SPRING & NEAP TIDES
Dates in red are SPRINGS
Dates in blue are NEAPS

SEPTEMBER

Time m	Time m
1 0447 0.7 / 1025 6.4 / W 1703 1.0 / 2237 6.7	**16** 0421 1.0 / 0958 6.3 / TH 1633 1.1 / 2207 6.5
2 0522 0.9 / 1059 6.3 / TH 1737 1.2 / 2312 6.4	**17** 0454 1.0 / 1030 6.3 / F 1707 1.1 / 2241 6.4
3 0555 1.1 / 1129 6.1 / F 1810 1.5 / 2344 6.1	**18** 0527 1.1 / 1103 6.3 / SA 1742 1.3 / 2315 6.3
4 0625 1.5 / 1157 5.8 / SA 1841 1.8	**19** 0601 1.3 / 1135 6.1 / SU 1818 1.5 / 2351 6.0
5 0013 5.7 / 0654 2.0 / SU 1225 5.5 / 1914 2.2	**20** 0639 1.7 / 1211 5.8 / M 1900 1.9
6 0045 5.3 / 0727 2.4 / M 1258 5.1 / ◐ 1955 2.6	**21** 0033 5.6 / 0723 2.2 / TU 1257 5.4 / ◐ 1954 2.3
7 0126 4.8 / 0811 2.9 / TU 1348 4.8 / 2057 3.0	**22** 0132 5.1 / 0825 2.6 / W 1405 5.1 / 2112 2.6
8 0242 4.4 / 0927 3.2 / W 1524 4.5 / 2243 3.1	**23** 0309 4.8 / 1001 2.9 / TH 1556 4.9 / 2258 2.6
9 0456 4.4 / 1126 3.2 / TH 1723 4.6	**24** 0508 4.9 / 1147 2.7 / F 1733 5.2
10 0020 2.8 / 0615 4.8 / F 1244 2.8 / 1826 5.0	**25** 0029 2.1 / 0625 5.4 / SA 1300 2.2 / 1839 5.7
11 0117 2.4 / 0702 5.2 / SA 1335 2.4 / 1910 5.4	**26** 0130 1.6 / 0719 5.8 / SU 1355 1.7 / 1931 6.1
12 0200 2.0 / 0740 5.5 / SU 1415 2.0 / 1949 5.8	**27** 0220 1.2 / 0804 6.2 / M 1441 1.4 / 2016 6.5
13 0238 1.6 / 0816 5.8 / M 1451 1.7 / 2025 6.1	**28** 0304 1.0 / 0844 6.4 / TU 1522 1.1 / ○ 2056 6.7
14 0313 1.3 / 0851 6.1 / TU 1525 1.4 / ● 2100 6.3	**29** 0342 0.9 / 0920 6.5 / W 1559 1.1 / 2133 6.7
15 0347 1.1 / 0925 6.2 / W 1559 1.2 / 2134 6.4	**30** 0417 0.9 / 0953 6.5 / TH 1633 1.1 / 2207 6.6

OCTOBER

Time m	Time m
1 0448 1.1 / 1023 6.3 / F 1704 1.3 / 2238 6.3	**16** 0427 1.0 / 1002 6.5 / SA 1643 1.0 / 2217 6.5
2 0518 1.3 / 1050 6.2 / SA 1734 1.5 / 2307 6.0	**17** 0503 1.1 / 1037 6.4 / SU 1721 1.2 / 2256 6.3
3 0546 1.7 / 1116 5.9 / SU 1803 1.9 / 2335 5.7	**18** 0541 1.4 / 1114 6.2 / M 1802 1.5 / 2337 6.0
4 0614 2.1 / 1141 5.6 / M 1833 2.2	**19** 0622 1.8 / 1155 5.9 / TU 1848 1.9
5 0003 5.2 / 0645 2.5 / TU 1211 5.2 / 1910 2.6	**20** 0026 5.5 / 0713 2.3 / W 1248 5.5 / ◐ 1948 2.3
6 0041 4.8 / 0725 3.0 / W 1254 4.8 / ◐ 2003 3.0	**21** 0134 5.1 / 0824 2.8 / TH 1404 5.1 / 2113 2.5
7 0149 4.5 / 0833 3.3 / TH 1418 4.5 / 2144 3.2	**22** 0321 4.9 / 1008 2.9 / F 1554 5.0 / 2255 2.4
8 0418 4.4 / 1042 3.3 / F 1640 4.6 / 2337 2.9	**23** 0503 5.1 / 1140 2.6 / SA 1719 5.3
9 0541 4.7 / 1209 3.0 / SA 1749 4.9	**24** 0013 2.1 / 0607 5.5 / SU 1243 2.2 / 1818 5.7
10 0040 2.5 / 0627 5.1 / SU 1259 2.5 / 1834 5.3	**25** 0110 1.7 / 0655 5.8 / M 1334 1.8 / 1907 6.1
11 0123 2.0 / 0705 5.6 / M 1339 2.1 / 1913 5.8	**26** 0156 1.4 / 0737 6.1 / TU 1417 1.5 / 1950 6.3
12 0201 1.6 / 0742 5.9 / TU 1416 1.8 / 1951 6.1	**27** 0236 1.2 / 0814 6.3 / W 1456 1.3 / 2029 6.4
13 0238 1.3 / 0817 6.2 / W 1453 1.4 / 2028 6.4	**28** 0313 1.2 / 0849 6.4 / TH 1531 1.3 / ○ 2104 6.4
14 0314 1.1 / 0853 6.4 / TH 1530 1.1 / ● 2104 6.5	**29** 0345 1.2 / 0920 6.3 / F 1604 1.3 / 2137 6.3
15 0351 0.9 / 0927 6.5 / F 1606 1.0 / 2140 6.6	**30** 0416 1.4 / 0948 6.3 / SA 1635 1.4 / 2207 6.1
	31 0446 1.6 / 1016 6.1 / SU 1705 1.6 / 2237 5.9

NOVEMBER

Time m	Time m
1 0515 1.9 / 1043 5.9 / M 1735 1.9 / 2306 5.6	**16** 0529 1.5 / 1102 6.3 / TU 1754 1.4 / 2333 6.0
2 0545 2.2 / 1111 5.6 / TU 1806 2.2 / 2338 5.3	**17** 0617 1.9 / 1150 6.0 / W 1847 1.7
3 0618 2.6 / 1146 5.3 / W 1843 2.5	**18** 0027 5.6 / 0714 2.3 / TH 1247 5.6 / 1949 2.1
4 0018 4.9 / 0658 2.9 / TH 1228 5.0 / 1931 2.8	**19** 0136 5.2 / 0825 2.6 / F 1401 5.3 / ◐ 2106 2.3
5 0119 4.6 / 0758 3.2 / F 1337 4.7 / ◐ 2047 3.0	**20** 0305 5.1 / 0951 2.7 / SA 1527 5.2 / 2228 2.3
6 0304 4.5 / 0933 3.3 / SA 1523 4.6 / 2227 2.9	**21** 0427 5.2 / 1109 2.5 / SU 1643 5.3 / 2337 2.1
7 0438 4.7 / 1106 3.0 / SU 1647 4.9 / 2340 2.6	**22** 0530 5.4 / 1211 2.3 / M 1743 5.6
8 0535 5.1 / 1207 2.6 / M 1742 5.2	**23** 0036 1.9 / 0620 5.7 / TU 1303 2.0 / 1835 5.8
9 0034 2.2 / 0619 5.5 / TU 1254 2.2 / 1828 5.6	**24** 0124 1.7 / 0704 5.9 / W 1349 1.8 / 1920 6.0
10 0118 1.8 / 0700 5.9 / W 1337 1.8 / 1911 6.0	**25** 0206 1.6 / 0743 6.0 / TH 1429 1.6 / 2001 6.0
11 0200 1.4 / 0739 6.2 / TH 1419 1.4 / 1953 6.3	**26** 0243 1.6 / 0818 6.1 / F 1506 1.6 / ○ 2038 6.1
12 0241 1.2 / 0818 6.4 / F 1501 1.2 / ● 2035 6.5	**27** 0318 1.6 / 0852 6.1 / SA 1540 1.6 / 2113 6.0
13 0322 1.1 / 0857 6.6 / SA 1542 1.1 / 2117 6.5	**28** 0351 1.7 / 0923 6.1 / SU 1613 1.6 / 2146 5.9
14 0403 1.1 / 0937 6.5 / SU 1624 1.0 / 2200 6.5	**29** 0424 1.8 / 0953 6.0 / M 1645 1.7 / 2218 5.8
15 0445 1.2 / 1018 6.5 / M 1708 1.1 / 2245 6.3	**30** 0456 2.0 / 1024 5.9 / TU 1718 1.9 / 2250 5.6

DECEMBER

Time m	Time m
1 0528 2.2 / 1056 5.7 / W 1751 2.1 / 2325 5.4	**16** 0616 1.7 / 1148 6.2 / TH 1844 1.4
2 0603 2.4 / 1132 5.5 / TH 1828 2.3	**17** 0025 5.8 / 0710 2.0 / F 1242 5.9 / 1940 1.7
3 0005 5.1 / 0643 2.7 / F 1214 5.2 / 1911 2.5	**18** 0122 5.5 / 0809 2.2 / SA 1340 5.6 / ◐ 2039 2.0
4 0056 4.9 / 0733 2.8 / SA 1307 5.0 / 2006 2.6	**19** 0224 5.3 / 0912 2.4 / SU 1444 5.4 / 2142 2.2
5 0201 4.8 / 0837 2.9 / SU 1415 4.9 / ◐ 2114 2.7	**20** 0330 5.2 / 1020 2.5 / M 1550 5.3 / 2248 2.3
6 0316 4.9 / 0951 2.9 / M 1529 5.0 / 2227 2.6	**21** 0435 5.2 / 1126 2.5 / TU 1656 5.2 / 2350 2.3
7 0425 5.0 / 1102 2.7 / TU 1637 5.1 / 2332 2.3	**22** 0535 5.3 / 1226 2.3 / W 1758 5.3
8 0522 5.3 / 1203 2.3 / W 1736 5.4	**23** 0047 2.2 / 0628 5.5 / TH 1319 2.2 / 1852 5.5
9 0031 2.0 / 0613 5.7 / TH 1257 2.0 / 1830 5.7	**24** 0137 2.1 / 0714 5.7 / F 1405 2.0 / 1939 5.6
10 0123 1.7 / 0701 6.0 / F 1348 1.6 / 1921 6.0	**25** 0220 2.0 / 0756 5.8 / SA 1446 1.9 / 2021 5.7
11 0212 1.4 / 0748 6.3 / SA 1437 1.3 / 2011 6.3	**26** 0259 2.0 / 0833 5.9 / SU 1523 1.7 / ○ 2059 5.8
12 0300 1.2 / 0834 6.5 / SU 1525 1.1 / ● 2101 6.4	**27** 0336 1.9 / 0908 5.9 / M 1559 1.7 / 2134 5.8
13 0348 1.2 / 0920 6.6 / M 1613 1.0 / 2150 6.4	**28** 0411 1.9 / 0940 6.0 / TU 1633 1.8 / 2207 5.8
14 0436 1.3 / 1008 6.5 / TU 1702 1.1 / 2240 6.3	**29** 0445 1.9 / 1013 5.9 / W 1707 1.8 / 2240 5.7
15 0525 1.5 / 1057 6.5 / W 1752 1.2 / 2332 6.1	**30** 0518 2.0 / 1046 5.9 / TH 1741 1.8 / 2314 5.6
	31 0552 2.1 / 1122 5.7 / F 1815 1.9 / 2351 5.5

YACHTMASTER EXERCISES FOR SAIL & POWER

EXTRACT 10: ST MALO TIDETABLE

TIME ZONE -0100
(French Standard Time)
Subtract 1 hour for UT
For French Summer Time add ONE hour in **non-shaded areas**

FRANCE – ST MALO
LAT 48°38'N   LONG 2°02'W
TIMES AND HEIGHTS OF HIGH AND LOW WATERS

SPRING & NEAP TIDES
Dates in red are SPRINGS
Dates in blue are NEAPS

MAY

#	Time m	#	Time m
1 SA	0413 9.7 / 1103 3.5 / 1650 10.0 / 2326 3.3	**16** SU	0517 10.8 / 1205 2.7 / 1740 10.9
2 SU	0505 10.6 / 1158 2.6 / 1736 10.9	**17** M	0029 2.7 / 0600 11.1 / 1247 2.5 / 1818 11.2
3 M	0021 2.4 / 0553 11.4 / 1248 1.9 / 1820 11.6	**18** TU	0108 2.5 / 0637 11.3 / 1324 2.3 / 1852 11.4
4 TU	0111 1.7 / 0638 12.1 / 1336 1.4 / 1902 12.2	**19** W	0143 2.3 / 0712 11.3 / 1356 2.3 / 1924 11.5
5 W	0158 1.3 / 0721 12.5 / 1421 1.1 / 1943 12.5	**20** TH	0215 2.3 / 0745 11.3 / 1427 2.3 / 1955 11.5
6 TH	0243 1.0 / 0804 12.7 / 1503 1.1 / 2023 12.6	**21** F	0245 2.4 / 0815 11.2 / 1456 2.5 / 2024 11.4
7 F	0325 1.1 / 0846 12.5 / 1525 1.4 / 2104 12.4	**22** SA	0314 2.5 / 0845 10.9 / 1525 2.8 / 2054 11.1
8 SA	0405 1.5 / 0928 12.0 / 1622 2.0 / 2146 11.8	**23** SU	0344 2.8 / 0915 10.6 / 1555 3.2 / 2124 10.7
9 SU	0447 2.1 / 1014 11.3 / 1703 2.8 / 2233 11.1	**24** M	0414 3.2 / 0948 10.1 / 1627 3.7 / 2158 10.2
10 M	0532 2.8 / 1106 10.4 / 1752 3.6 / 2329 10.2	**25** TU	0448 3.7 / 1026 9.6 / 1704 4.2 / 2239 9.7
11 TU	0628 3.6 / 1211 9.6 / 1856 4.3	**26** W	0530 4.1 / 1114 9.1 / 1753 4.6 / 2334 9.2
12 W	0047 9.6 / 0741 4.1 / 1335 9.2 / 2022 4.5	**27** TH	0626 4.4 / 1220 8.8 / 1859 4.8
13 TH	0215 9.5 / 0906 4.0 / 1500 9.4 / 2143 4.2	**28** F	0050 9.0 / 0740 4.5 / 1342 8.8 / 2020 4.7
14 F	0331 9.8 / 1018 3.6 / 1606 9.9 / 2249 3.6	**29** SA	0209 9.2 / 0901 4.2 / 1456 9.2 / 2135 4.1
15 SA	0429 10.3 / 1117 3.1 / 1657 10.5 / 2342 3.1	**30** SU	0318 9.8 / 1011 3.6 / 1559 9.9 / 2239 3.4
		31 M	0419 10.4 / 1113 2.9 / 1653 10.6 / 2338 2.7

JUNE

#	Time m	#	Time m
1 TU	0514 11.1 / 1210 2.3 / 1744 11.4	**16** W	0031 3.1 / 0608 10.5 / 1247 3.0 / 1823 10.9
2 W	0037 2.1 / 0606 11.7 / 1304 1.8 / 1833 11.9	**17** TH	0111 2.9 / 0647 10.7 / 1325 2.9 / 1859 11.1
3 TH	0130 1.6 / 0656 12.1 / 1354 1.5 / 1920 12.3	**18** F	0147 2.8 / 0723 10.8 / 1401 2.8 / 1933 11.2
4 F	0221 1.3 / 0746 12.2 / 1442 1.5 / 2006 12.4	**19** SA	0222 2.7 / 0757 10.8 / 1435 2.8 / 2006 11.2
5 SA	0309 1.3 / 0834 12.1 / 1528 1.7 / 2053 12.3	**20** SU	0257 2.7 / 0831 10.8 / 1509 2.9 / 2040 11.1
6 SU	0356 1.5 / 0922 11.8 / 1614 1.9 / 2140 11.9	**21** M	0331 2.8 / 0905 10.6 / 1544 3.0 / 2114 10.9
7 M	0442 2.0 / 1011 11.3 / 1700 2.7 / 2230 11.3	**22** TU	0407 3.0 / 0941 10.4 / 1620 3.2 / 2151 10.6
8 TU	0531 2.5 / 1102 10.7 / 1750 3.3 / 2324 10.7	**23** W	0444 3.2 / 1019 10.1 / 1659 3.6 / 2231 10.3
9 W	0623 3.1 / 1157 10.1 / 1846 3.8	**24** TH	0525 3.5 / 1101 9.8 / 1743 3.9 / 2316 10.0
10 TH	0025 10.1 / 0720 3.6 / 1259 9.6 / 1949 4.1	**25** F	0611 3.7 / 1150 9.5 / 1834 4.1
11 F	0132 9.8 / 0823 3.9 / 1408 9.5 / 2055 4.1	**26** SA	0010 9.7 / 0705 3.9 / 1248 9.3 / 1935 4.1
12 SA	0241 9.7 / 0926 3.9 / 1515 9.6 / 2158 3.9	**27** SU	0115 9.6 / 0809 3.9 / 1357 9.4 / 2044 4.0
13 SU	0343 9.8 / 1025 3.7 / 1612 9.9 / 2255 3.6	**28** M	0226 9.8 / 0920 3.7 / 1507 9.7 / 2155 3.6
14 M	0438 10.1 / 1118 3.4 / 1702 10.3 / 2345 3.3	**29** TU	0335 10.1 / 1031 3.3 / 1614 10.3 / 2302 3.1
15 TU	0526 10.3 / 1205 3.2 / 1745 10.6	**30** W	0442 10.6 / 1137 2.8 / 1716 10.9

JULY

#	Time m	#	Time m
1 TH	0007 2.5 / 0544 11.1 / 1238 2.3 / 1813 11.5	**16** F	0048 3.3 / 0629 10.3 / 1304 3.2 / 1842 10.7
2 F	0109 2.0 / 0642 11.5 / 1336 2.0 / 1907 12.0	**17** SA	0130 3.0 / 0709 10.6 / 1345 3.0 / 1919 11.0
3 SA	0206 1.6 / 0737 11.8 / 1430 1.7 / 1958 12.2	**18** SU	0209 2.8 / 0746 10.8 / 1424 2.8 / 1955 11.2
4 SU	0300 1.4 / 0829 12.0 / 1521 1.7 / 2047 12.3	**19** M	0247 2.6 / 0821 10.9 / 1501 2.7 / 2030 11.3
5 M	0351 1.4 / 0917 11.9 / 1609 1.8 / 2134 12.1	**20** TU	0325 2.4 / 0856 11.0 / 1538 2.6 / 2104 11.4
6 TU	0438 1.6 / 1003 11.6 / 1654 2.2 / 2220 11.7	**21** W	0401 2.4 / 0930 11.0 / 1614 2.6 / 2139 11.3
7 W	0522 2.0 / 1047 11.1 / 1738 2.7 / 2304 11.2	**22** TH	0437 2.5 / 1005 10.8 / 1650 2.8 / 2215 11.0
8 TH	0604 2.6 / 1130 10.6 / 1821 3.2 / 2350 10.6	**23** F	0513 2.7 / 1041 10.5 / 1727 3.1 / 2254 10.7
9 F	0646 3.2 / 1215 10.0 / 1906 3.8	**24** SA	0551 3.1 / 1120 10.0 / 1808 3.4 / 2336 10.3
10 SA	0041 9.9 / 0731 3.8 / 1307 9.6 / 1958 4.2	**25** SU	0633 3.4 / 1206 9.6 / 1857 3.8
11 SU	0139 9.5 / 0824 4.1 / 1410 9.3 / 2100 4.4	**26** M	0031 9.9 / 0726 3.8 / 1307 9.5 / 2000 4.0
12 M	0248 9.4 / 0927 4.3 / 1520 9.3 / 2206 4.3	**27** TU	0142 9.6 / 0836 3.8 / 1425 9.5 / 2119 4.0
13 TU	0356 9.6 / 1031 4.2 / 1625 9.6 / 2307 4.0	**28** W	0305 9.5 / 0958 3.8 / 1549 9.8 / 2239 3.6
14 W	0456 9.5 / 1129 3.9 / 1718 10.0	**29** TH	0426 10.0 / 1116 3.4 / 1704 10.3 / 2351 2.8
15 TH	0000 3.6 / 0546 9.9 / 1220 3.5 / 1803 10.4	**30** F	0538 10.6 / 1226 2.7 / 1807 11.2
		31 SA	0100 2.2 / 0639 11.3 / 1328 2.2 / 1902 11.9

AUGUST

#	Time m	#	Time m
1 SU	0200 1.6 / 0732 11.8 / 1424 1.7 / 1951 12.4	**16** M	0157 2.5 / 0730 11.1 / 1412 2.5 / 1940 11.6
2 M	0254 1.2 / 0820 12.1 / 1514 1.4 / 2037 12.6	**17** TU	0236 2.2 / 0805 11.4 / 1450 2.2 / 2015 11.8
3 TU	0341 1.1 / 0903 12.1 / 1558 1.4 / 2119 12.5	**18** W	0313 1.9 / 0839 11.6 / 1526 1.9 / 2049 12.0
4 W	0423 1.2 / 0943 12.0 / 1638 1.7 / 2158 12.2	**19** TH	0348 1.8 / 0912 11.6 / 1600 1.9 / 2122 11.9
5 TH	0500 1.6 / 1020 11.6 / 1713 2.2 / 2235 11.6	**20** F	0422 1.9 / 0944 11.5 / 1634 2.2 / 2155 11.7
6 F	0533 2.1 / 1055 11.0 / 1745 2.9 / 2310 10.8	**21** SA	0454 2.2 / 1017 11.2 / 1707 2.6 / 2229 11.2
7 SA	0603 3.0 / 1129 10.3 / 1817 3.6 / 2348 10.0	**22** SU	0526 2.7 / 1051 10.7 / 1743 3.1 / 2307 10.7
8 SU	0635 3.7 / 1207 9.7 / 1856 4.3	**23** M	0602 3.3 / 1132 10.1 / 1826 3.7 / 2355 9.9
9 M	0035 9.2 / 0719 4.3 / 1300 9.1 / 1953 4.8	**24** TU	0651 4.0 / 1229 9.5 / 1928 4.3
10 TU	0145 8.7 / 0824 4.7 / 1422 8.7 / 2116 5.0	**25** W	0112 9.2 / 0803 4.4 / 1401 9.2 / 2058 4.4
11 W	0318 8.6 / 0950 4.8 / 1554 8.9 / 2237 4.7	**26** TH	0257 9.2 / 0944 4.4 / 1546 9.4 / 2232 3.9
12 TH	0436 9.0 / 1105 4.1 / 1659 9.5 / 2340 4.1	**27** F	0430 9.7 / 1113 3.7 / 1704 10.3 / 2348 2.9
13 F	0530 9.6 / 1202 3.9 / 1746 10.1	**28** SA	0539 10.6 / 1224 2.9 / 1803 11.3
14 SA	0032 3.5 / 0614 10.2 / 1250 3.4 / 1827 10.7	**29** SU	0057 2.1 / 0633 11.4 / 1323 2.1 / 1853 12.1
15 SU	0116 2.9 / 0653 10.7 / 1333 2.9 / 1904 11.2	**30** M	0152 1.4 / 0720 12.0 / 1413 1.5 / 1937 12.6
		31 TU	0239 1.0 / 0802 12.4 / 1458 1.2 / 2018 12.8

98

EXTRACT 11: ST MALO TIDAL CURVE

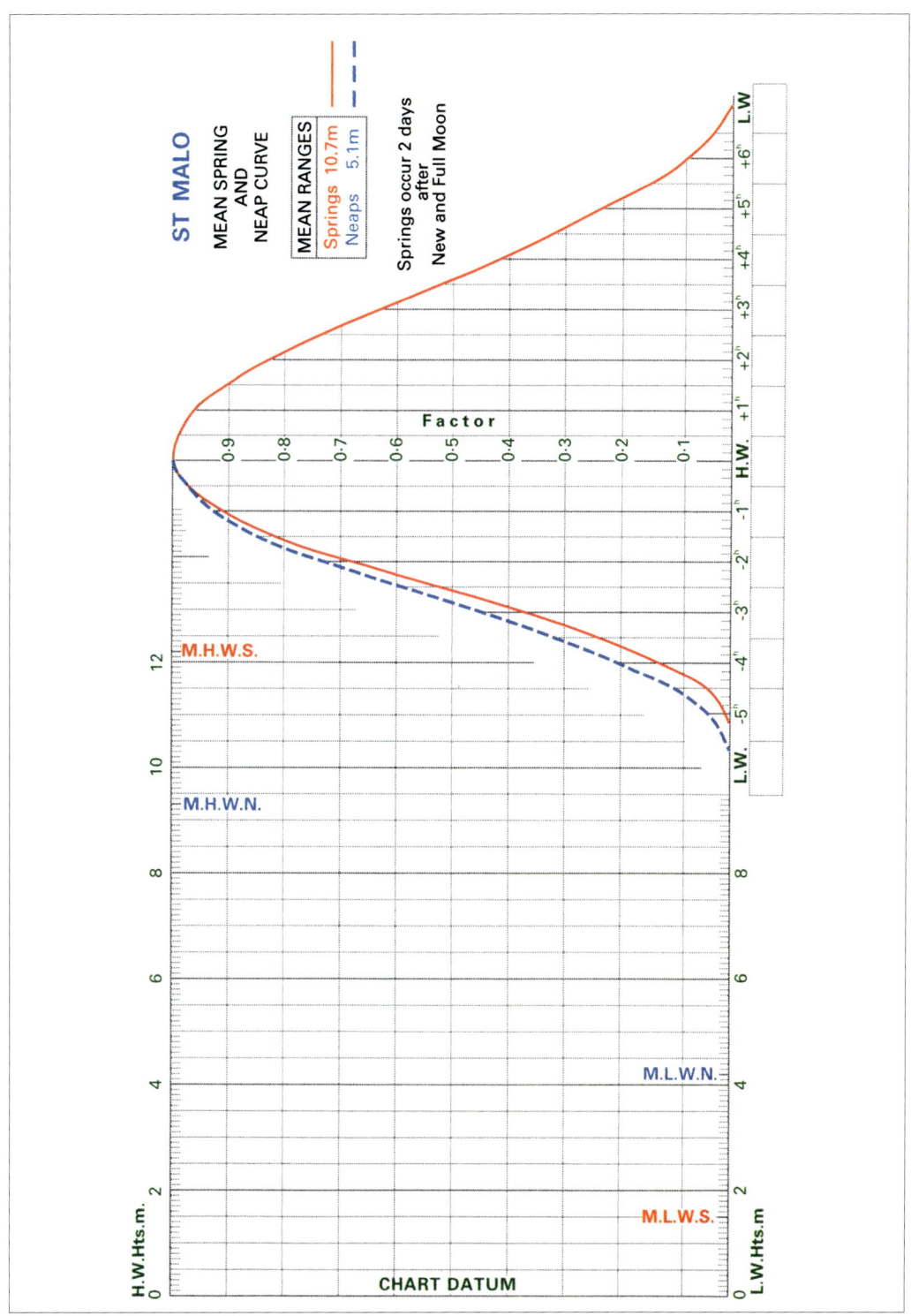

EXTRACT 12: PORT INFORMATION – ST MALO

ST MALO

SHELTER Two options: 1. Lock into Bassin Vauban, min depth 6m. Excellent shelter near the walled city. Berth on pontoon marked for your LOA; no fingers; no turning room. Bassin Duguay-Trouin, beyond bridge, is better for long stay. No ⚓ in basins; 3kn speed limit. Outside the lock 3 waiting buoys are N of appr chan; keep clear of vedette and Condor berths.
Lock operates five times in each direction, ie
      Inbound: HW –2½, –1½, –½, HW+½, +1½.
      Outbound: HW–2, –1, HW, +1, +2.
Assistance is given with warp-handling; pas de problème.
Lock sigs are IPTS Nos 2, 3 and 5. In addition:
🟡 next to the top lt means both lock gates are open; main message is the same, but beware current. Freeflow operation is rare due to busy road traffic over rolling bridge.
🔴🔴 over 🟢 = all movements prohib, except big ship departure.
2. Good shelter nearer St Servan in Bas Sablons marina, entered over sill 2m above CD. Two W waiting buoys outside. Depth of water over sill is shown on a digital gauge atop the bkwtr, visible only from seaward; inside, a conventional gauge at base of bkwtr shows depths <3m. ⓥ berths are 32-66 (E side) and 43-75 (W side) of pontoon A, and 92-102 and 91-101 on pontoon B. N end of both pontoons are exposed to fresh NW winds.
At **Dinard** there is a yacht ⚓ and moorings, reached by a beaconed chan, all dredged 2m, but virtually full of local boats.

NAVIGATION WPT 48°41´·38N 02°07´·28W [SWM buoy, Iso 4s Whis], 127°/1·9M to Grand Jardin lt, where in fresh W'lies it can be quite rough. Care is needed due to many dangerous rks around the appr chans, plus strong tidal streams. The 3 main chans (see also 9.18.4) are:
1. Petite Porte (130°/129°); best from N or NW and at night.
2. Grande Porte (089°/129°); from the W and at night.
These 2 chans meet at Le Grand Jardin lt and continue 129°.
3. La Grande Conchée (181·5°); most direct from N, but unlit.

LIGHTS AND MARKS See chartlets and 9.18.4.

R/T *St Malo Port* Ch **12** 16 (H24). Marinas Ch 09.

TELEPHONE
ST MALO: Port HM 02·99·20·63·01, fax 02·99·56·48·71; HM (Vauban) 02·99·56·51·91; HM (Bas Sablons) 02·99·81·71·34; Aff Mar 02·99·56·87·00; CROSS 02·98·89·31·31; SNSM 02·98·89·31·31; ⊖ 02·99·81·65·90; Météo 02·99·46·10·46; Auto 08.92.68.08.35; Police 02·99·81·52·30; ℍ 02·99·56·56·19; Brit Consul 02·99·46·26·64.

FACILITIES
ST MALO: **Bassin Vauban** (250 + 100 ⓥ) ☎ 02·99·56·51·91, 🗎 02·99·56·57·81, €2.67, C (1 ton); **Société Nautique de la Baie de St. Malo** ☎ 02·99·40·84·42, 🗎 02·99·56·39·41, Bar (ⓥ welcome).
ST SERVAN: **Marina Les Bas-Sablons** (1216 + 64 ⓥ on pontoon A, berths 43-75 and 32-64) ☎ 02·99·81·71·34, 🗎 02·99·81·91·81, €2.22, Slip, C, BH (10 ton), Gaz, R, YC, Bar, P & D pontoon 'I'; Note: Pumps are operated by French credit card; see HM. **Services:** El, Ⓔ, ME, CH, ✕, C, BY, SM, SHOM. **Town** Gaz, 🚆, R, Bar, ✉, Ⓑ, ⇌, ✈ (Dinard). Ferry: Portsmouth, Poole or Jersey.

DINARD: **HM** ☎ 02·99·46·65·55, Slip, ⚓, M €1.91 (afloat) €1.25 (drying), P, D, L, temp AB; **YC de Dinard** ☎ 02·99·46·14·32, Bar; **Services:** ME, El, Ⓔ, ✕, M, SM. **Town** P, D, ME, El, CH, 🚆, Gaz, R, Bar, ✉, Ⓑ, ⇌, ✈. ⊖ 02·99·46·12·42; ℍ 02·99·46·18·68.

EXTRACT 13: PORT INFORMATION – ST PETER PORT

ST PETER PORT

TIDES –0439 Dover; ML 5·2; Duration 0550; Zone 0 (UT)

NOTE: St Peter Port is a Standard Port, see Tide Tables overleaf.

To find depth of water over the sill into Victoria marina:
1. Look up predicted time and height of HW St Peter Port.
2. Enter table below on the line for height of HW.
3. Extract depth (m) of water for time before/after HW.

Ht (m) of HW St Peter Port	Depth of Water in metres over the Sill (dries 4·2 m)						
	HW	±1hr	±2hrs	±2½hrs	±3hrs	±3½hrs	±4hrs
6·20	2·00	1·85	1·55	1·33	1·10	0·88	0·65
·60	2·40	2·18	1·75	1·43	1·10	0·77	0·45
7·00	2·80	2·52	1·95	1·53	1·10	0·67	0·25
·40	3·20	2·85	2·15	1·63	1·10	0·57	0·05
·80	3·60	3·18	2·35	1·73	1·10	0·47	0·00
8·20	4·00	3·52	2·55	1·83	1·10	0·37	0·00
·60	4·40	3·85	2·75	1·93	1·10	0·28	0·00
9·00	4·80	4·18	2·95	2·03	1·10	0·18	0·00
·40	5·20	4·52	3·15	2·13	1·10	0·08	0·00
·80	5·60	4·85	3·35	2·23	1·10	0·00	0·00

SHELTER Good, especially in Victoria Marina which has a sill 4·2m above CD, with a gauge giving depth over sill. Access approx HW±2½ according to draft; see Table above. R/G tfc lts control ent/exit. Appr via buoyed/lit chan along S side of hbr. Marina boat will direct yachts to waiting pontoon or ❶ pontoons with FW (nos 1-5) N of the waiting pontoon. Pontoons for tenders are each side of marina ent. Local moorings are in centre of hbr, with a secondary fairway N of them. ⚓ prohib. ❶ berths in Queen Elizabeth II and Albert marinas by prior arrangement.

NAVIGATION WPT 49°27'·82N 02°30'·78W, 227°/0·68M to hbr ent. Offlying dangers, big tidal range and strong tidal streams demand careful navigation. Easiest appr from N is via Big Russel between Herm and Sark, passing S of Lower Hds SCM lt buoy. The Little Russel is slightly more direct, but needs care especially in poor visibility; see 9.19.5 and 9.19.9 chartlet. From W and S of Guernsey, give Les Hanois a wide berth. Beware ferries and shipping. Hbr speed limits: 6kn from outer pier heads to line from New Jetty to Castle Cornet; 4kn W of that line.

An **RDF beacon**, GY 304·50kHz, on Castle Bkwtr is synchronised with the co-located horn* to give distance finding. The horn blast begins simultaneously with the 27 sec long dash following the four GY ident signals. Time the number of seconds from the start of the long dash until the horn blast is heard, multiply by 0·18 = your distance in M from the horn; several counts are advised.

LIGHTS AND MARKS Outer ldg lts 220°: Front, Castle bkwtr hd Al WR 10s (vis 187°–007°) Horn 15s*; rear, Belvedere Oc 10s 61m 14M, intens 217°-223°. By day, White patch at Castle Cornet in line 223° with Belvedere Ho (conspic). Inner Ldg lts 265°: Front, Oc R 5s; rear, Iso R 2s, vis 260°–270° (10°). This ldg line is for the use of ferries berthing at New Jetty. It extends through moorings in The Pool, so must not be used by yachts which should appr Victoria marina via the buoyed/lit S channel (dashed line).

Traffic Signals on White Rock (N) pierhead:
- 🔴 (vis from seaward) = No entry.
- 🔴 (vis from landward) = No exit (and at New Pier, SW corner).

These sigs do not apply to boats, <15m LOA, under power and keeping clear of the fairways.

R/T St Peter Port Marina Ch M 80 (office hrs). Monitor St Peter Port Control VHF Ch **12** (H24) but call Port Control if necessary when within the pilotage area. Water taxi Ch 10 (0800-2359LT). Call St Peter Port Radio CRS Ch 20 for safety traffic. Link calls Ch 62. St Sampson Ch 12 (H24).

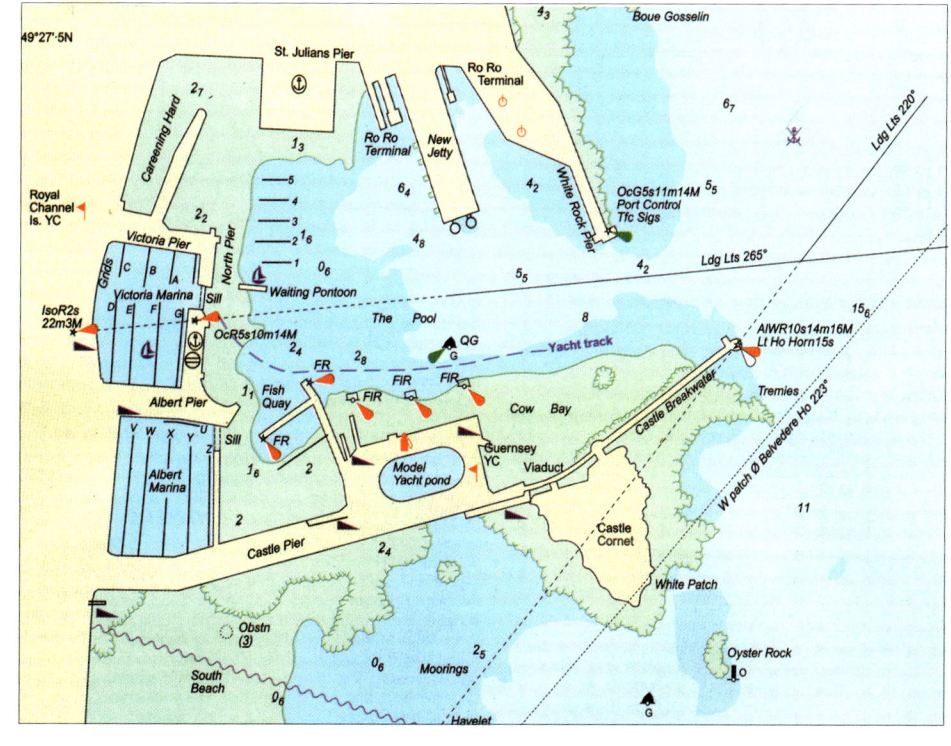

YACHTMASTER EXERCISES FOR SAIL & POWER

EXTRACT 14: PORT INFORMATION – GRANVILLE AND ÎLES CHAUSEY

GRANVILLE

Manche **48°49'·91N 01°35'·97W** ❋❋❋❋❋❋

CHARTS AC 3656, *3659*, 3672; SHOM 7156, 7341; ECM 534, 535; Imray C33B; Stanfords 16, 26

TIDES –0510 Dover; ML 7·1; Duration 0525; Zone –0100

Standard Port ST-MALO

Times				Height (metres)			
High Water		Low Water		MHWS	MHWN	MLWN	MLWS
0100	0800	0300	0800	12·2	9·3	4·2	1·5
1300	2000	1500	2000				
Differences REGNÉVILLE-SUR-MER							
+0010	+0010	+0030	+0020	+0·4	+0·3	+0·2	0·0
GRANVILLE							
+0005	+0005	+0020	+0010	+0·7	+0·5	+0·3	+0·1
CANCALE							
–0002	–0002	+0010	+0010	+0·8	+0·6	+0·3	+0·1

SHELTER Good in the marina, Port de Hérel, 1·5–2·5m. Caution: at ent sharp turn restricts visibility. Access over sill HW –2½ to +3½. Depth over sill shown on lit digital display atop S bkwtr: eg 76=7·6m; 00 = no entry; hard to read in bright sun. The Avant Port (dries) is for commercial/FVs.

NAVIGATION WPT 48°49'·34N 01°37'·09W, 055°/0·95M to S bkwtr lt. Beware rks off Pte du Roc, La Fourchie and Banc de Tombelaine, 1M SSW of Le Loup lt. Appr is rough in strong W winds. Ent/exit under power; speed limit 4kn, 2kn in marina. WCM buoy, VQ (9) 10s Whis, marks Le Videcoq Rk drying 0·8m, 3½M W of Pte du Roc.

LIGHTS AND MARKS Hbr ent is 0·6M E of Pte du Roc (conspic), Fl (4) 15s 49m 23M, grey tr, R top. No ldg lts, but S bkwtr hd on with TV mast leads 055° to ent. Best appr at night is with Le Loup bearing 085° to avoid pot markers off Pte du Roc; hbr lts are hard to see against town lts. Turn port at bkwtr to cross the sill between R/G piles, Oc R/G 4s. Sill of bathing pool to stbd is marked by 5 R piles, Fl Bu 4s.

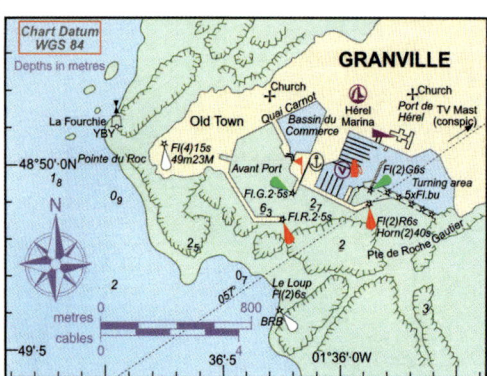

R/T Port VHF Ch 12 16 (HW±1½). Marina Ch 09, H24 in season.

TELEPHONE HM (Port) 02·33·50·17·75; Aff Mar 02·33·91·31·40; CROSS 02·33·52·72·13; SNSM 02·33·61·26·51; ⊖ 02·33·50·19·90; Météo 02·33·22·91·77; Auto 08.92.68.08.50; Police 02·33·50·01·00; Dr 02·33·50·00·07; Hosp 02·33·90·74·75; Brit Consul 02.99.46.26.64.

FACILITIES Hérel Marina (850+150 visitors) ☎ 02·33·50·20·06, ⛽ 02·33·50·17·01, €1.86, ⚓ pontoon G (1st to stbd), Slip, P, D, ME, BH (12 ton), C (10 ton), CH, Gaz, ⌂, ⚒, Bar, SM, El, ✕, ⚓; **YC de Granville** ☎ 02·33·50·04·25, ⛽ 02·33·50·06·59, L, M, BH, D, P, CH, ⚒, Slip FW, AB, Bar; **Services:** CH, M, ME, El, ⓔ, ✕, SHOM, SM. **Town** P, D, ME, ⚒, Gaz, R, Bar, ⌂, ⓑ, ✈, → (Dinard). www.granville.cci.fr. Ferry: UK via Jersey or Cherbourg.

ILES CHAUSEY

Manche **48°52'·14N 01°49'·09W** S ent ❋❋❋❋❋

CHARTS AC 3656, *3659*; SHOM 7156, 7155, 7161, 7134; ECM 534, 535; Imray C33B; Stanfords 16, 26

TIDES –0500 Dover; ML 7·4; Duration 0530; Zone –0100

Standard Port ST-MALO

Times				Height (metres)			
High Water		Low Water		MHWS	MHWN	MLWN	MLWS
0100	0800	0300	0800	12·2	9·3	4·2	1·5
1300	2000	1500	2000				
Differences ILES CHAUSEY (Grande Ile)							
+0005	+0005	+0015	+0015	+0·8	+0·7	+0·6	+0·4

SHELTER Good except in strong NW or SE winds. Grande Ile is not a French Port of Entry; it is privately owned, but may be visited. Moor fore-and-aft to W ⚓s, free; some dry at sp. Very crowded Sat/Sun in season, especially as drying out in Port Homard (W side of Grande Ile) is actively discouraged. Note the tidal range when ‡ing or picking up ⚓. Tidal streams are not excessive.

NAVIGATION WPT 48°51'·44N 01°48'·57W, 332°/1·2M to La Crabière lt. The S route into the Sound is easy, via access chan marked by a SHM lt buoy, ECM & WCM bns. The N route requires adequate ht of tide, SHOM 7134 or detailed SDs for transits, and/or local knowledge, but is not too difficult. No access 1/4 to 30/6 to bird sanctuary, all areas E of line from lt ho to L'Enseigne.

LIGHTS AND MARKS Grande Ile lt ho, Fl 5s, is conspic. La Crabière, Oc WRG 4s 5m 9/6M, Y bn; W sector leads into sound; see 9.18.4. By day, La Crabière on with L'Enseigne, W bn tr, B top (19m), leads 332°. From N, L'Enseigne on with Grande Ile lt ho leads 156° to La Grande Entree.

R/T None. **TELEPHONE** Police 02·33·52·72·02; CROSS 02·33·52·72·13; Auto 08.92.68.08.50; SNSM 02.33.50.28.33.

FACILITIES Village FW & ⚒ (limited), Gaz, R, Bar, L, ⌂. Ferry to UK via Granville and Jersey.

EXTRACT 15: PORT INFORMATION – DIÉLETTE

DIÉLETTE

Manche, **49°33´·24N 01°51´·89W** ✿✿✿✿✿✿

CHARTS AC *3653*; SHOM 7158, 7133; ECM 528, 1014; Imray C33A; Stanfords 16

TIDES HW –0430 on Dover (UT); ML 5·4m

Standard Port ST-MALO

Times				Height (metres)			
High Water		Low Water		MHWS	MHWN	MLWN	MLWS
0100	0800	0300	0800	12·2	9·3	4·2	1·5
1300	2000	1500	2000				
Differences DIÉLETTE							
+0045	+0035	+0020	+0035	–2·5	–1·9	–0·7	–0·3

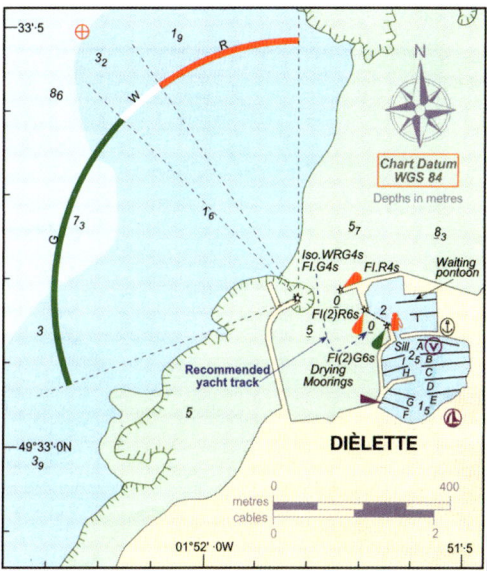

SHELTER Good in marina, but some scend near HW when retaining wall covers. Do not attempt entry in strong W'lies. Outer hbr entr dredged to CD +0.5m; accessible for 2.5m draft with Coefficient > 55. W side of outer hbr dries approx 5m (local moorings). Enter marina, about HW±3 for 1·5m draft, over a sill with lifting gate 4m above CD; waiting pontoon outside.

NAVIGATION WPT 49°33´·49N 01°52´·24W, 140°/0·40M to W bkwtr lt. Appr is exposed to W'ly winds/swell. Caution: rky reef dries close NE of appr; cross tide at hbr ent. From/to the S keep seaward of WCM lt buoy off Flamanville power stn.

LIGHTS AND MARKS Power stn chys (72m) are conspic 1·2M to SW. Dir lt 140°, Iso WRG 4s 12m 10/7M, W tr/G top at hd of West bkwtr, vis G070°-135°, W135°-145° (10°), R145°-180°; on same tr is a lower lt, Fl G 4s 6m 2M. Other lts as chartlet.

R/T VHF Ch 09; summer 0800-1300, 1400-2000LT; winter 0900-1200, 1330-1800LT.

TELEPHONE ☎ 02·33.23.34.02; Aff Mar 02·33.23.36.00; Météo 08·92·68·08·50; CROSS 02·33.52.72.13; SNSM 02·33.04.93.17; YC 02·33·93·10·24.

FACILITIES Marina (370+70 ✓), 02·33.53.68.78, 📠 02·33.53.68.79; €2.19, D, P, Slip, C (30 ton); Ferry to Cl. **Village**, Bar, R. Also facilities at Flamanville (1·3M).

YACHTMASTER EXERCISES FOR SAIL & POWER

EXTRACT 16: DEVIATION CURVE

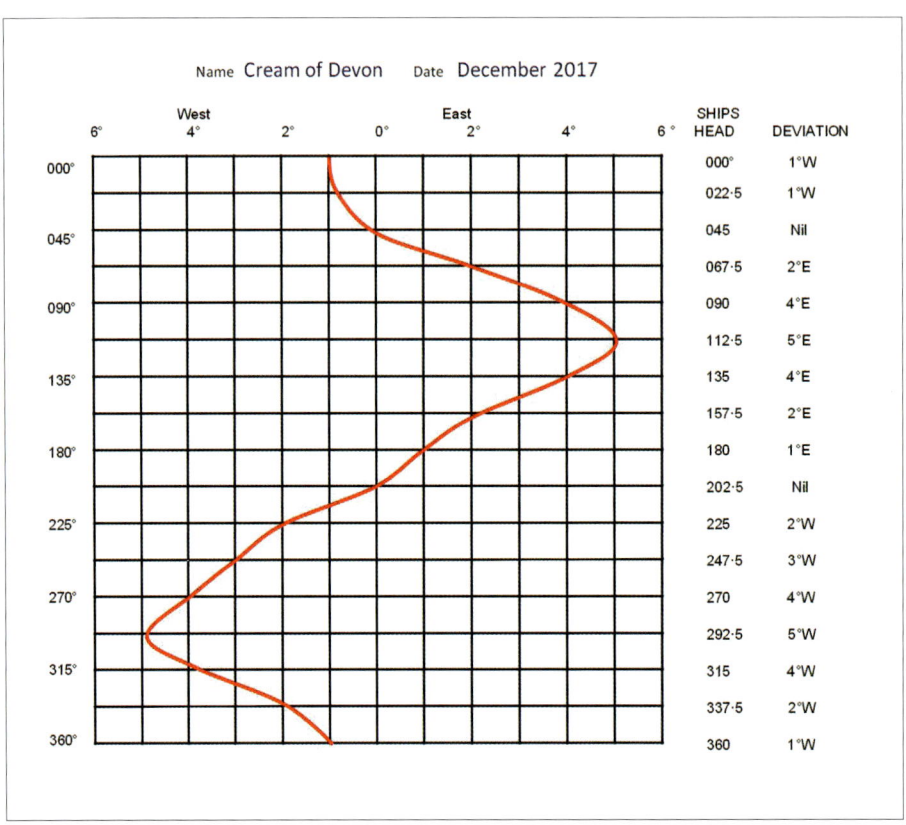

SHIPS HEAD	DEVIATION
000°	1°W
022·5	1°W
045	Nil
067·5	2°E
090	4°E
112·5	5°E
135	4°E
157·5	2°E
180	1°E
202·5	Nil
225	2°W
247·5	3°W
270	4°W
292·5	5°W
315	4°W
337·5	2°W
360	1°W

EXTRACT 17: TIDAL DIFFERENCES FOR CHERBOURG–BARFLEUR

Standard Port CHERBOURG

Times				Height (metres)			
High Water		Low Water		MHWS	MHWN	MLWN	MLWS
0300	1000	0400	1000	6·4	5·0	2·5	1·1
1500	2200	1600	2200				
Differences BARFLEUR							
+0110	+0055	+0052	+0052	+0·1	+0·3	0·0	0·0